The cover design mainly consists of an image painted by the author.

The Path

As portrayed in the image, the path is centered and rhythmic, which is essential in order for one to remain instinctually related. This is always the case even when the journey traverses high peaks and low valleys as depicted here. The goal is the transparent Self, which is found on the lower right side of the image.

PROPHETS IN
OUR MIDST

PROPHETS IN OUR MIDST

JUNG, TOLKIEN, GEBSER,
SRI AUROBINDO AND THE MOTHER

DAVID T. JOHNSTON, PH.D.

PROPHETS IN OUR MIDST
JUNG, TOLKIEN, GEBSER, SRI AUROBINDO AND THE MOTHER

iUniverse books may be ordered through booksellers or by contacting:

iUniverse
1663 Liberty Drive
Bloomington, IN 47403
www.iuniverse.com
1-800-Authors (1-800-288-4677)

ISBN: 978-1-5320-0954-9 (sc)
ISBN: 978-1-5320-0955-6 (e)

Print information available on the last page.

iUniverse rev. date: 05/17/2017

To the Mother

TABLE OF CONTENTS

PREFACE

I have written the essays in this book over a long period of time, without ever considering the possibility of having them published. Nor did I write any of the essays with the other ones in mind. I wrote them because of an intense interest in the subject matter as expressed in each essay and in order to gain further appreciation and understanding myself. As time went on, I became aware of the possibilities of the internet, and I simply placed them on my web site, without any further thought. Now I am aware of the world of self-publishing, and I am motivated to collate four of my essays that I can now see relate to the future in something of a parallel way, even though they involve different authors and different angles of approach. I present them here in the event others will find their messages of interest as I did, and further their own explorations on the material presented here.

INTRODUCTION

Since the dawn of the Age of Aquarius in 1926, if not prior to it, there has been a descent of new integral consciousness on earth that is revolutionizing everything. According to Sri Aurobindo and the Mother, in January 1956, the Supermind or Truth consciousness itself has become active in the world play, implying that Truth is penetrating into the complexities of world affairs. This can explain the fact that world events become stirred up and the tensions exacerbated until there is an unforeseen resolution that seems to promote increasing balance and justice. The lives and teachings of Sri Aurobindo and the Mother are most closely aligned to the new consciousness that is at work in the world today, although others, more or less consciously, have also become involved in creatively relating to it. Of prime importance, especially in the West, is C. G. Jung, the most significant pioneer of Western psychology, whose teachings and life both go a long way towards fulfilling the human demands made by this new consciousness. I have selected two other figures from Western culture, J R. R. Tolkien and Jean Gebser, whose creative work can be described as expressing something of this new consciousness as well.

Being a genuine prophet refers to any individual who speaks with the word of God. The prophet is an inspired seer, capable of expressing the Will of God. Sri Aurobindo has been identified by the Mother as the Avatar of our times, who incarnated as a direct act of Will of the Supreme, and Sri Aurobindo proclaims her to be the Divine Mother, with transcendent, universal and individual dimensions of being. As Avatar and Divine Mother, they naturally possess powerful qualities of far seeing Prophets of the new consciousness, which they not only bring into vision, but also most completely embody. C. G. Jung also embodies much of this new consciousness in both his life and work, which not only consists of a highly intuitive visionary dimension, but also an important aspect of praxis as well.

There are genuine prophetic voices and indications today that exist in precisely the same way as they existed during the time of the prophets in Jewish history and elsewhere at all times. As has always been the case regarding prophetic inspirations, there is considerable resistance to the prophetic messages, which, today, are effectively identical, at least inasmuch as deep social change depends on the far-reaching process of individuation of selected individuals. In the contemporary world, this resistance is largely due to the highly organized nature of life and the misplaced belief in the primacy of conscious intent and will. As is ever the case, we could all benefit from understanding the prophetic voice today and pay heed to its message. I write this, realizing that by far the majority of people today do not believe that there is such a thing as a true prophet and certainly not one that relates to the life of our times.

The basic message today, as in the past, is that there is a need for cultural renewal, which happens by way of individuals and society connecting, both in ideals and dynamic living, with the evolving archetypal substratum of the psyche. The archetypal psyche is the region where one can forge a relationship with the fundamental ways of apprehending and living evolutionary life and life's basic patterns, which exist behind everyday life as we know and experience it. In other words, we need to relate directly to the manifest god, which, in Judeo-Christian terms, refers to a renewed and conscious covenant with the transcendent God who is in harmony with the deeper demands of the times. In order to gain some understanding of what that refers to today, I allude to the works of the spiritual leaders, Sri Aurobindo and the Mother, the psychologist, C. G. Jung, J. R. R. Tolkien, especially in reference to his masterpiece, *The Lord of the Rings*, and Jean Gebser, the author of a fascinating book on the evolution of consciousness.

SRI AUROBINDO AND THE MOTHER

For the most insightful understanding on where the evolution of consciousness is leading today, I turn to Sri Aurobindo, who was born in Calcutta, India on August 15, 1972 and the Mother, who was born in Paris, France, on February 21, 1878, as Mirra Alfassa. Sri Aurobindo spent the age of 7 to 21 in England from 1879-1893, in the final years, studying at King's College, Cambridge. The Mother studied occultism in Tlemcen Algeria beginning in 1905 for two years with the occultists Max Theon and his wife. She subsequently lived in Japan for almost four years from 1916-1920, taking up residence in the Ashram in Pondicherry on April 24, 1920. Beginning in November 1926, the Mother took over the full spiritual and material responsibilities for Ashram affairs.

Sri Aurobindo understands consciousness to be fundamentally evolving in an ascending spiral-like fashion, although he also articulates a particular arrow of development from the Irrational Age to the Age of Reason taking place in an upward linear direction. His perspective fully embraces both the feminine and the masculine principles. The evolution of consciousness, in his view, begins at a spiritual high point, the Symbolic Age, from where it degenerates to the Typal Age with its ethical leanings. From there, the mind proceeds downward to the Conventional Age, where convention through dogma, doctrine and tradition reigns. The aspiration for truth calls up the Age of Reason, which plays the important role of challenging convention. But reason doesn't suffice and the Subjective Age responds, first as false subjectivity as in the current narcissistic-ordered world, then true subjectivity and genuine spirituality.

Sri Aurobindo interwove a vision that not only recognizes a spiral-like descent from the Symbolic Age to the present, but also an ascending order from the Irrational Age through the Age of Reason to the Subjective Age, which we are presently engaged in, if only at the beginning. In the process, he articulates an inspiring world view that includes potential spiritual transformation of different cultural attitudes and of life itself. This is directly in line with Jung's view of the individuation process; although the latter never systematically developed the effect of the individuation process on culture, it underlies everything he writes. Like Jung, Sri Aurobindo emphasizes the important role of individuals to first undergo a creative process of change, in order for society to eventually undergo the same process.

In the Subjective Age, humans have the divine task of increasing consciousness in order to participate in the creation of a New World. In place of alienation and meaningless existence, the end effect of the modern and post-modern minds Jung, like Sri Aurobindo, appeals to humans to become more conscious and to participate in the creation of the world, where the psychoid nature (which includes and transcends spirit and matter) of the archetype makes the physical aspect of the transformation possible. In fact, Sri Aurobindo's spiritual companion, the Mother, insists that the new consciousness must have the capacity to change the world's physical conditions in order to render it an entirely new creation. She actually claims that the new creation already exists side by side with the old one and that it is simply a matter of accessing it.

Regarding Sri Aurobindo's and the Mother's supramental yoga, which is integral to the establishment of the New World, although it needs to be distinguished from it, it is essential to surrender to *That* beyond form and the cosmic mind. This act of surrender, as they understand it, does not result in loss of consciousness, but brings in Truth, the Mother of All and the creative source of life, who potentially makes manifest the Supreme Will. In fact, it leads to full embodiment of the Supreme Will and direct involvement in the new divine creation in time. Thus, the power of becoming, which is most evident in unending time, is in the process of becoming transformed. Here, it is noteworthy that Jung identified with Aion, the god of endless time, and then detached from him, suggesting a relationship with this transformed power of becoming.

The essential structural ground of Reality is based on the symbolic number four. Qualitatively, four relates to wholeness and completion, and the incarnated Self. In Jung's view it is a very important number and a symbol for individuation and wholeness of being. According to Sri Aurobindo, the Supermind and source of Truth is based on the number four. The number four is also a fundamental theme running throughout *The Lord of the Rings,* suggesting that it is the basic structural ground and deeper foundational reality of the epic. In the West, and in the contemporary scientific world, we think more quantitatively, which has its own validity, but psychologically and spiritually we need to see numbers qualitatively and not merely as a measure of quantity. So, for instance, the constellation of the number four in the psyche through a dream or authentic fantasy means that compensatory wholeness is potentially emerging into consciousness in order to bring harmony and balance to a relatively one-sided way of being.

C. G. JUNG

C. G. Jung was born in Basel, Switzerland on July 26, 1875. He travelled considerably in his adult life, including to east Africa in 1925, to England in 1920, 23, and 1925, to India and Ceylon in 1937-38, and to the United States in 1924-25, which included a visit with the Taos Pueblo people, and again in 1936-37. His opus is principally concerned with the individuation of individuals, although it also refers to the individuation of culture, especially Western Culture. That both levels of the psyche are addressed by his work, even though he emphasizes the individual is possible because, at the archetypal level, the microcosm and the macrocosm are effectively one. In fact, Jung often directly addresses the needs of Western culture and the modern mind and a citation honoring him at the *Federal Technical Institute* in Zurich, where he taught for several years, refers to his work and describes him as having interpreted the primal symbols and mankind's individuation. Jung's prophetic contribution to our culture and our times is reflected in this reference although he, himself never refers to the individuation of mankind per se. Not only do Jung's works have a major theoretical component, but an important dimension of praxis also permeates his work throughout.

Jung empirically observed the spontaneous activity of the unconscious, always with a salutary effect when the contents were assimilated to consciousness. The goal of his approach to therapy is individuation and the individuation process, which means finding and becoming conscious of one's unique path to wholeness. Fundamentally, this refers to two factors; developing a personal relationship to the archetypal psyche, especially the central archetype, the Self, and the increasing differentiation of one's nature.

The archetypes refer to the way one apprehends the world and dynamically live in the world. They are the fundamental blueprints for action and the instinct's self-perception. Individuals living in harmony with the archetypes are living in instinctual harmony, which, when one is involved in the individuation process can become conscious. Individual's living consciously in relationship with the archetype of the Self, the centre of the psyche, live in relationship with their wholeness along with a spiritual connection to the infinite.

These archetypes are, in fact, great formative powers that seek realization, powers that can no longer abide residing in the ethereal air of idealism in relationship not only of individuals but of culture in general. In more practical terms, individuation refers to the instinctive drive to differentiate all four functions of consciousness, thinking, feeling, sensation and intuition as well as the two attitudes, introversion and extraversion. It can also be understood as the individualization of one's soul-type as priest, leader, trader and servant, each of which requires some differentiation of all qualities of being, all functions of consciousness and attitudes.

According to mythical accounts, the final stage of the heroic journey requires individual heroes to bring the boon or treasure back home so that others and the community can profit by it. In the case of Jung, he found vehicles to communicate his findings in the Grail tradition, alchemy and Gnosticism, allowing him to explain his experiences in a way that is understandable to individuals on the path of conscious individuation. Near the end of his life, despite some resistance and with the help of Aniela Jaffé, he also wrote an 'autobiography' entitled *Memories, Dreams, Reflections* that has influenced countless numbers of average folk. Moreover, based on a dream, where he saw himself standing on top of a hill delivering his message to the average person, who *understood* what he was saying, he also wrote a piece for a book, which he also organized and edited, called *Man and his Symbols*.

Jung's specific prophetic message advances the path of conscious individuation to clearly include full spiritual transformation as an accessible phenomenon in what he refers to as the coming Age of the Holy Spirit, in which he foresees a state of Oneness of the Holy Spirit, and the conscious restoration of oneness of the unconscious. This vision parallels the supramental manifestation as understood by Sri Aurobinbdo and the Mother. Attaining that level of consciousness requires reconciling the most extreme opposites of good and evil, and complete abolition of the individual ego. Not considering Sri Aurobindo's and the Mother's path of Integral Yoga, Jung's path is new, more thorough and comprehensive than in the past and includes opening, through the *unus mundus* (one world) and synchronicity (meaningful coincidences), to new acts of creation in time. Jung's final depiction of the Self is a highly differentiated static and dynamic model, consisting of fourfold quaternities and reflects detachment from the power of becoming.

J. R.R. TOLKIEN

J. R. R. Tolkien was born to British parents on January 02, 1892, in Bloemfontein, Orange Free State, now a part of South Africa, and returned to England in 1895 with his mother and younger brother, Hilary. Tolkien's creative life was recognizably influenced by a recurrent dream of a Great Wave that rolled over trees and green meadows, and from which he woke gasping for breath. He recounted that the dream came with a memory, and he referred to it as his 'Atlantis-haunting' dream, implying relatedness to the distant ancestral past of Atlantis and pagan mythology. The dream gradually subsided through his creative writing, although the legend of Atlantis and the Great Wave, subtly underscore his whole legendarium.

The redemption of paganism is revealed by the fact that, in terms of virtues, *The Lord of the Rings* is imbued with Christian values, such as the four cardinal virtues of the Middle Ages, prudence, justice, fortitude and temperance as well as honor, obedience and faithfulness. Moreover, an important ingredient in everybody's individual development in the story is moral choice, free will and self-sacrifice, and this in the context of an ordered universe. Needless to say, as well as beneficent choice based on integrity of purpose, free-will can lead to inferior moral choice, perhaps even for evil. In fact, there are many examples of both types of choice in *The Lord of the Rings,* as well as the consequences.

By and large, in the pre-Christian and pre-classical pagan world, the gods/goddesses ruled; the supreme ruler in ancient Greece being Zeus, and the then current belief was that the best course in life was to bow to one's fate, which was ultimately Zeus' Will. In Nordic countries the supreme god was Wotan or Odin, where a similar dynamic held rule. In either case, there was cosmic order but no free will, the belief being that the stars ruled destiny and one was obliged to submit to the procession of the gifts and poisons of *heimarmene* or fate.

One of the eventual outcomes of the rejection of the pagan worldview was repression of the gods/goddesses, which coincide with the repression of archetypal and instinctive aspects of a full life. The gods and goddesses became diseases, and, in the contemporary world, they also manipulate us in increasingly sophisticated way through propaganda, advertising, public relations and other means of dominating the play of life. Although we believe in free will and moral choice, we have, as a culture, little sense of cosmic order, and virtually no conscious recognition of its existence and the implications. Nonetheless, I believe that more people have some experience of it through synchronicity than is generally acknowledged.

Synchronicities or meaningful coincidences, where inner and outer worlds are in evident harmony, are conscious personal experiences of cosmic order or general acausal orderdness, which involves new creations in time and the initiative of a higher will. *The Lord of the Rings* is full of such synchronicities, examples of personal experiences of cosmic order; yet the role of free will and moral choice is never abrogated. One particularly fine example takes place when, at the council of Elrond, where the fate of the Ring of Power was discussed by representatives of Free People, Frodo made a free choice to become the Ring-bearer, despite his declaration that he did not know the way.

In fact Tolkien's beautiful creation myth at the beginning of the *Silmarillian*, depicts fundamental order in the universe, which includes gods, goddesses, and angelic beings, some of which fall, or become fallen, elves and humans, hence both forces for good and evil forces will mal intent. The Lord of the Rings is a human story about relinquishing ambition through the ring of power, where almost everybody is tempted from the Merlin-like figure, Gandalf to the human hobbits, Bilbo and Frodo. Running parallel to this eventuality is a great battle between these two contradictory forces of good and evil.

As I mention above, *The Lord of the Rings* is fundamentally structured on the symbolic number four, a leitmotif that runs through the entire epic. The Shire, the hobbits home town, is partitioned into four. There are four hobbits that go on the heroic quest. From a Jungian perspective, they can be understood as representing four functions of consciousness, Frodo, the intuitive type and superior function, Merry, the thinking type, Pippin the sensation type and inferior function, and Sam, the feeling type. Frodo and Sam seem to be introverted, while Merry and Pippin are extraverted. From Sri Aurobindo's perspective, there are four different soul-types, priest, leader, trader and servant, where Tolkien depicts these specific soul-types as primarily embodied in Gandalf the wizard (priest), Aragorn the King, Frodo, the bourgeois [trader] and his servant Sam, who wins the day through love, Eros and feeling. From a psychological and spiritual perspective, the epic depicts individuation of all these main personalities through psychic (incarnated soul) transformation and, in the case of Gandalf, spiritualization in his transformation from Gandalf the Grey to Gandalf the White.

There is one other character that is worthy of mention in regard to the number four, Tom Bombadil, who has existed since the beginning of time. He is fatherless, thus the original man or *Anthropos,* who stands four feet tall and three feet wide, and who is unaffected by the ring of power. Whereas four means wholeness, three refers to insight and process, and represents a second qualitatively important number, that is embodied by this interesting figure.

The quest comes to an end with Frodo relinquishing the Ring of Power, with the help of his shadow, Gollum. The final battle between good and evil ends with a victory for the good, and the epic ends with the union of opposites, for example elves and dwarves, humans and the values of the spiritual world through the wizard, Gandalf, and humans, elves, dwarves and the Wild Men of the woods. Humankind finds redemption, primarily depicted in Aragorn, known as Elessar (Elfstone), becoming King of the two Kingdoms along with his beautiful elf-wife, Arwen Evenstar, as Queen. Of particular significance is the renaissance of the Shire, especially under the servant, Sam's, leadership and his planting seeds of cultural renewal. On a symbolic level, there is both the individuation of individuals but also the (subtle) physical establishment of the New World.

JEAN GEBSER

Jean Gebser was born on August 20, 1905 in the Prussian city of Posen, which now belongs to Poland, and, after much travelling, he settled near Bern, Switzerland in 1939. He puts the theory of the evolution of consciousness on a firm foundation given his references to historical evidence. From the point of view of this study there are, in particular, four major points of interest. The first is that the origin is always present. The second is that there are, from time to time, quantum mutations in consciousness that originate from the source or ever-present origin. The third is that a major transformation in consciousness is taking place today, as evidenced in a wide variety of disciplines. Fourth, the new integral consciousness is transparent to the Self and recaptures the essence of all previous structures of consciousness. In addition, time has entered the world as a subjective force, rendering the experience of the new consciousness as intense, emotionally authentic, and concrete, while remaining open to the truth of being.

Gebser substantiates the theory of the evolution of consciousness, including the fact that we are currently in the process of a major transformation of consciousness, with much historical evidence. He also gives considerable insight on the nature of five different structures of consciousness, beginning with the time of origins and the archaic structure of consciousness through to the magical structure, the mythological structure, the mental structure and the present integral structure of consciousness. He consequently supports Sri Aurobindo's and Jung's interest in the individuation of humankind and the individuation process or transformation of consciousness that is taking place today. Moreover, his observations on the different structures of consciousness are insightful and psychologically sophisticated. In particular, his views on the new integral structure of consciousness strike me as an interesting variation in perspective that parallels both Sri Aurobindo's and Jung's observations. In fact, Gebser acknowledged the similarities between his thought on the evolution of consciousness and Sri Aurobindo's view and, living in Switzerland from 1939 on, it is highly likely that he met Jung or, at least, was exposed to his thinking as well.

I am especially referring here to Gebser's claim that the new integral structure of consciousness involves both truth and transparency to archetypal energies along with their realization in concrete reality and integration by ego consciousness. This position has similarities with Jung's understanding that both consciousness and dynamic nature are based on an archetypal foundation, which is psychoid, meaning that it both embraces and transcends spirit and matter. Moreover, supporting Gebser's view on the subjectivity of time and intensity, the archetype has feeling-tone and its constellation comes with emotional intensity and the potential for integration into ego consciousness.

*   *   *

There has been a descent of a new integral consciousness roughly since the beginning of the twentieth century, if not the end of the nineteenth century. This descending process changes everything including the way life is apprehended, organized and dynamically lived. All four of the individuals I have discussed have to some degree understood the nature of this change in consciousness and the implications. Their prophetic messages educate us on the nature of the transformation being asked of us today. Sri Aurobindo, along with his collaborator, the Mother, as well as Jung, not only give us a comprehensive intuitive vision about the New World being born, but psychological and spiritual praxis on how to realize this new vision. Sri Aurobindo and the Mother are particularly comprehensive and far seeing in their vision for the future of humanity. The essays in this book reflect the thought of all four of these pioneers.

JUNGIAN LIGHTS ON SRI AUROBINDO'S *SAVITRI*: A MYTH FOR OUR TIME

David Johnston

ABSTRACT

Sri Aurobindo is a master yogi and visionary and writes brilliantly in various areas of culture. He considers himself to be primarily a poet by vocation. His poetry finds its apotheosis in the epic poem *Savitri*, a work in excess of 23,000 lines. The principal theme involves the heroine, Savitri's, descent into the realm of the Lord of Death in order to release her soul-mate, Satyavan, and to return together with him into life. The poem, in fact, is about the essential nature of many aspects of spiritual, psychological and even physical realities. It is a symbolic myth and mantra reflecting Sri Aurobindo's own felt-experiences and understanding. It is his *magnum opus* and the most complete expression of his worldview and vision in that it involves the whole person. According to him, as a mantra, it has the capacity of transforming the individual's inner consciousness. As a symbol, it represents the truth behind what is represented in the poem -- the release of the truth of being from the clutches of death into life. *Savitri* is a meaningful answer to the cry for a guiding myth or worldview that can be heard behind the chaotic noise of the contemporary world.

JUNGIAN LIGHTS ON SRI AUROBINDO'S *SAVITRI*: A MYTH FOR OUR TIME

INTRODUCTION

Sri Aurobindo was born in 1872 in Calcutta and educated in England between the ages of seven and twenty, at which time he returned to his native country, India. Some 10-15 years prior Gandhi's revolutionary activities, he was a principal participant in the revolution that liberated India from British rule and is considered to be a national hero. He has wide-ranging cultural interests and writes with breathtaking insights in several different areas. Culturally, he is primarily a poet, with his poetry finding it's apotheosis in *Savitri*, an epic poem, which he wrote and re-wrote over many years. Sri Aurobindo is also a master yogi and seer and presents the world with an unparalleled vision for individual and world transformation based on spiritual principles and an active spiritual life. On his own account, his vision finds its most complete expression in the above-mentioned poem. Sri Aurobindo's spiritual collaborator, the Mother, actively participated in his work and contributes to it, what might be called, an insistence on the material realization of his vision. This includes active administration of the Sri Aurobindo ashram and the initial realization of Auroville, the city of the Dawn, located in South India. She brings complementary feminine values, reflected in Sri Aurobindo's vision, to his masculine emphasis.

Sri Aurobindo's work is becoming more accessible to the Western mind, which is growing increasingly intuitive and open to ideas from the East. His Cambridge education and knowledge of English culture permeate his writings, including *Savitri*, making his work attractive to Westerners. He is a consummate master of written English, imbuing it with great power and beauty. *Savitri* is a symbolic myth and mantric poem that can give people direct felt-experience and imagery of spiritualized energy that is essential for the full redemption and transformation of contemporary life.

THE NEED FOR A VISION AND THE CRY FOR MYTH

My intention here is to briefly reflect upon Sri Aurobindo's *magnum opus, Savitri,* which he himself declares is both a legend and a symbol.[1] By legend is meant a traditional story about heroic or notorious figures that is considered to have historical reference; in this case, its origin is found in the *Vedas,* India's source scriptures, and which later was given form as a human tale in the *Mahabharata.* As symbol, Sri Aurobindo's rendition penetrates to the truth behind and represented by the legend. *Savitri* is, in fact, a great mythic poem and an archetypal expression of what is involved in humankind's potential self-fulfillment. It consists of descriptions of underlying behavior patterns for a spiritually fulfilled and completely individuated life. The Mother, Sri Aurobindo's spiritual collaborator, goes so far as to contend that "it is the prophetic history of the earth, embodying in itself the fulfillment of man's life on earth.[2]"

The following lines from the poem are indicative of the scope and beauty of Sri Aurobindo's vision:

> *O Sun-Word, Thou shalt raise the earth-soul to Light*
> *And bring down God into the lives of men;*
> *Earth shall be my work-chamber and my house*
> *My garden of life to plant a seed divine.*
> *The mind of earth shall be a home of light,*
> *The life of earth a tree growing towards heaven,*
> *The body of earth a tabernacle of God.[3]*

---

[1] Sri Aurobindo, 1970b
[2] As reported in Purani, 1967, p. 2
[3] *Savitri,* Book XI, Canto one, p. 699

In a letter to a young man, the eminent psychologist C. G. Jung expresses similar sentiments although with more emphasis on the psychological requirements for the fulfillment of Sri Aurobindo's vision. In it, he writes: "One must be able to suffer God. That is the supreme task for the seeker of ideas. He must be the advocate of the earth. God will take care of himself. My principle is: *Deus et homne*. God needs man in order to become conscious just as he needs limitation in time and space. Let us therefore be for him limitation in time and space, an earthly tabernacle.[4]" If Sri Aurobindo's vision depicts a metaphysical divine fiat, then Jung's letter outlines the necessary human response for its realization.

According to Jung, the appropriate myth today for contemporary individuals is the myth of consciousness, perhaps better understood as the myth of Gnosis, knowledge of the Self. This ultimately involves becoming conscious of all psychological opposites, including the masculine and feminine principles, good and evil and their reconciling synthesis. Jung describes this process in his great work, the *Mysterium Coniunctionis*.[5] It is noteworthy that the opposites referred to are not those of the personal complex-ridden psyche, nor the ego and non-ego or the Self, but the opposites in the godhead itself. Sri Aurobindo's poem *Savitri* is a poetic rendition of this very realization.

SAVITRI AS LEGEND AND SYMBOL

Briefly, the legend of *Savitri* involves a childless king, Aswapathy, propitiating the Mother of the universe for a son. She grants him his boon and the additional boon of a daughter, who is a portion of the universal Mother Herself. As the tale unfolds, his daughter, Savitri, after a long search, finds her soul-mate in Satyavan, the son of a dispossessed king, Dyumatsena. After one year together, Satyavan dies, as prophesied. Savitri then accompanies the Lord of Death to His realm and persuades him to allow her to return to life with her beloved.

---

[4]   quoted in Adler & Jaffé, 1973, p. 65
[5]   Jung, 1974 passim

According to Sri Aurobindo, as a symbol, the poem revolves around the following archetypal phenomena.[6] King Aswapathy represents human aspiration for the realization of a divine life. Savitri is the embodiment of a portion of the universal Mother, whose purpose for incarnation is to enable humankind to fulfill its prayers. She represents the Divine Word, which is born to save. Satyavan represents the soul, of which the essence is "the divine truth of being."[7] Dyumatsena symbolizes the Divine Mind, which has here fallen blind, losing not only its vision but its natural right to its heavenly kingdom.

Sri Aurobindo bases his symbolic rendition of *Savitri* on his own felt-experience, vision and understanding. The nature of the symbol for him is essentially the same as it is for Jung. The latter notes that it is a "sensuously perceptible expression of an inner experience," based on the transcendent function involving the reconciliation of opposites.[8] He describes it as a "'libido analogue'" that effectively canalizes instinctual energy into new form.[9] Likewise, Campbell defines the symbol as "an energy evoking and directing agent.[10]" He also approvingly quotes Thomas Merton, who observes that the "true symbol" "awakens ... consciousness to a new awareness of the inner meaning of life and of reality by way of affective relationship to one's "'deepest self.[11]'" The true symbol, in other words, is a vehicle for the spiritual transformation of consciousness and meaning.

THE CRY FOR MYTH IN THE CONTEMPORARY WORLD

The existentialist psychologist, Rollo May, wrote a book entitled *The Cry for Myth* where he expresses his conviction in the [urgent] need for myth in our day[12]. Living myth, according to both him and Campbell,

---

[6] 1972

[7] Ibid, p. 265

[8] Adler & Jaffé, 1973, p. 269

[9] Jung, 1967/1975, p. 48

[10] 1969/1990, p. 178

[11] quoted in Campbell, 1972/1973, p. 265

[12] 1991

contribute to a sense of individual and communal identity, as well as provide the foundation for a moral order.[13] In addition, they each contend, myth can awaken consciousness to the mystery of being or the *mysterium tremendum et fascinens* of the existential nature of the universe.

Sri Aurobindo's poem *Savitri* fulfills all these requirements for the New Age that is in the process of being born. The poem is, in fact, a dialogue between a highly individuated individual and the archetypal powers of the unconscious, fulfilling in a superlative fashion Jung's appeal for the need, today, for an active dialogue between the conscious and the collective unconscious. The result is a symbolic myth that speaks directly to what Sri Aurobindo refers to as the "Cosmic Self," that is the individual's innermost being, the microcosm, and the "general mind of man," the macrocosm. [14]

Campbell[15] likens mythologies and religions to great poems. The poet, according to Robert Graves, was originally a priest and seer, at least in the Celtic tradition.[16] This is also true of other traditions including the Hindu tradition, dating back to the time of the mantras of the Vedic cycle, some three to seven thousand years ago and perhaps beyond. Sri Aurobindo is a contemporary poet-seer and *Savitri* a high order mantric poem. The mantra consists of words of power that find their source deep within, while being "framed in the heart.[17]" According to Sri Aurobindo, its purpose is to "create vibrations in the inner consciousness" that encourage the realization of what the mantra symbolizes.[18] *Savitri*, in other words, is not only a visionary poem, but its mantric quality renders it a supreme vehicle for the transformation of consciousness and for a life organized around the Self.

Perhaps it is not correct to say that there is no coalescing myth or worldview that provides a focus for life today. But, if there is, it is a narrow

---

[13] 1975

[14] 1970b, p. 800

[15] 1973

[16] 1978

[17] Sri Aurobindo, quoted in Pandit, 1967/1970/1972, p. 35

[18] p. 35

one organized around materialistic science, technology, consumerism and the profit motive, somewhat modified by humanistic concerns. Moreover, as the industrial age gives way to the information age and the modern mind gives way to post-modernism, a centerless, open-ended relativistic world without reference to any authority is growing, where this solipsistic focus is being increasingly subjected to narcissistic individualism and the will to power. This comes along with the quantification of life, social isolation, mass-mindedness and alienation from the instincts and the power of symbols. It also encourages compartmentalization in both individual life and the life of the culture, where the left hand doesn't know or even care what the right hand is doing. Jung's observation that everywhere one hears the cry for a *Weltanschauung*, that is a meaningful worldview or philosophy of life, is more relevant today than ever.[19]

When a people's myth breaks down, life becomes fragmented and disoriented. This has always been the case, whether it be in the second and third century classical Greece, Egypt of three thousand BC or the Hebrew world of Isaiah. During the breakdown of classical Greece, Lucretius wrote that he could see "aching hearts in every home ...forced to vent themselves in recalcitrant repining.[20]" In Proverbs 29:18, we are warned that when there is no vision, people destroy themselves. It is not difficult for sensitive individuals to relate to both these observations today. Increasingly, people find life meaningless and without purpose, while defending themselves in all manner of ways, whether it be through mindless consumerism, obsessive involvement with new technology, or through excessive use of alcohol and drugs, whether legal or illicit. Add to this a popular culture of movies, music, television programs, video games, and endless possibilities on the internet that generally appeal to the lowest common denominator, while often celebrating destructive tendencies and shadow qualities, and the situation looks anything but hopeful.

People at all times have had a coalescing worldview that gives meaning

---

[19] 1967/1975, p. 337
[20] quoted in May, 1991, p. 16

to existence and focus to all activities of life and social patterns. At least, this is the case in normal times when society is functioning creatively and productively in tune with its ideals. The most recent period in Western consciousness of an integrated worldview dates back to the Middle Ages, when all life and art was organized around a Christian conception of life based on a geocentric universe. There was, however, considerable repression, which exploded with the Renaissance, the period when there was a creative shift in consciousness towards more direct concern and involvement with life in this extraverted world, along with the exaltation of the human ego. This coincided with a heliocentric conception of the universe and the beginnings of the development of the scientific mind and positivism or objective reason.

But today, not only has our thinking turned more subjective but science has given us a new view of the reality of the physical universe. Now the sun itself is perceived as but a star amongst billions of stars, and our universe a part of a galaxy of stars and planets, amongst millions of galaxies. Meanwhile, leading physicists have come to regard physical reality to be of a unitary nature. Likewise, in psychology, C.G. Jung has given evidence for the unitary nature of all reality, both physical in his conception of a *unus mundus* and the Self defined as both a spiritual and spiritual and physical unitary reality.[21]

The chaos of the present post-modern condition is giving birth to a deep-seated yearning for direction and purpose, integrated around a spiritual center and wholeness. There is a cry for a guiding myth and an integral *weltanschauung* that is in harmony with the most contemporary view of reality, and that does not repress life but fulfills it in all its multifacetedness. There is, in addition, growing awareness, especially among women, of a need for re-evaluation of the feminine, which in some quarters, is acknowledged as necessitating a return of the Goddess. As a mythic poem of the Goddess as heroine, who penetrates the Kingdom of death, and defeats death in order to release the soul and truth of being into

---

[21] 1967/1975

life, Sri Aurobindo's *Savitri* is a remarkable response to all these aspirations. It is a myth for our time.

*   *   *

Sri Aurobindo's epic poem, *Savitri*, is a symbolic myth that responds to a deeply felt need in the contemporary mind. Not only does it represent a world-view that is in harmony with the most recent understanding of scientific reality but, as a symbol, it penetrates to the essential truth of that reality. It concomitantly describes what is involved in the fulfillment of a spiritually individuated life. This is the goal of Jung's myth of consciousness for our time. Not only is *Savitri* a vision for individual and collective self-fulfillment but, as a mantra, it has a directly transformative effect on the inner consciousness. Such a magnificent poem calls for intelligent reflection.

REFERENCES

A. B. Purani (1977). Lectures on Savitri. Pondicherry: Sri Aurobindo Ashram.

Adler, G. & Jaffé, A. (Eds.). (1973). C.G. Jung: Letters: 1905-1950. (Vol. 1). (R.F.C. Hull, Trans.) Princeton, N.J.: Princeton University Press.

Campbell, Joseph (1973) Myths to live by. New York: Bantam Books (Original work published in 1972).

Campbell, Joseph (1975). The masks of god: Creative mythology. New York: The Viking Press, Inc.

Campbell, Joseph (1990). The flight of the wild gander. New York: Harper Collins Publishers. (Original work published 1969).

Graves, Robert (1978). The white goddess: A historical grammar of poetic myth. New York: Farrar Strauss and Giroux.

Jerusalem Bible, The (1966). Garden City, N.Y.: Doubleday & Company, Inc.

Jung, C.G. (1974). Mysterium coniunctionis. In R.F.C. Hull (Trans). The Collected Works of C.G. Jung. (Vol. 4). Princeton, NJ: Princeton University Press.

Jung, C.G. (1975). The structure and dynamics of the psyche. In R.F.C. Hull (Trans). The Collected Works of C.G. Jung. (Vol. 8, 2nd ed.). Princeton, N.J.: Princeton University Press. (Original work published 1967).

May, Rollo (1991). The cry for myth. New York: Bantam Doubleday Dell Publishing Group, Inc.

Pandit, M.P. (1971). Sri Aurobindo on the Tantra. Pondicherry, India: Dipti Publications. (Original work published in 1967.

Sri Aurobindo (1970a). *Savitri*: A legend and a symbol. In Sri Aurobindo Birth Centenary Library. (Vol. 28). Pondicherry, India: Sri Aurobindo Ashram Press.

Sri Aurobindo (1970b). *Savitri*: A legend and a symbol. In Sri Aurobindo Birth Centenary Library. (Vol. 29). Pondicherry, India: Sri Aurobindo Ashram Press.

Sri Aurobindo (1972). On himself. In Sri Aurobindo Birth Centenary Library, (Vol. 26). Pondicherry, India: Sri Aurobindo Ashram Press.

JUNG'S GNOSTIC CREATION MYTH: THE CREATIVE SHADOW PLEROMA, AND SRI AUROBINDO AND THE MOTHER

David Johnston

ABSTRACT

This essay is about Jung's Gnostic creation myth, which he wrote in 1916 as an important part of his encounter with the unconscious. He called it the *Seven Sermons to the Dead,* and attributed its writing to Philemon, a winged being he encountered in dreams and fantasies, who assumed the role of guru with superior insight. I refer to a Vedic creation myth commented on by Sri Aurobindo and a creation story of the Mother as well as relevant passages from Sri Aurobindo's *Savitri* for the sake of comparison. In all four cases there is a primordial creative Shadow and the number of principal beings [deities] is four, suggesting that the qualitative number four [4] is significant as a fundamental truth of existence and individual wholeness. Jung's myth puts more emphasis on the created world, while Sri Aurobindo's and the Mother's accounts tell a story as to how the original luminous fourfold being turned into its opposite. Jung writes that his early fantasies, including the one mentioned above, foreshadowed his entire life and scientific work as a psychologist. I work through each of the seven sermons and indicate their psychological meaning, while alluding to his developed approach to psychological. I also briefly analyze two seminal initiation dreams Jung had, one between the age of three [3] and four [4] and one at the age of thirty-seven [37]. The first dream is his initiation into the mystery of the earth, and the second his initiation into the wisdom of alchemical transformation through the Divine Mother as Sophia. I end this essay by discussing how the path of individuation involves both the psychic being or heart-Self centered transformation and spiritual ascension or spiritual transfiguration as indicated in Jung's early fantasies.

JUNG'S GNOSTIC CREATION MYTH: THE CREATIVE SHADOW PLEROMA, AND SRI AUROBINDO AND THE MOTHER

INTRODUCTION

The Mother counseled her audience with the observation that "we can choose from many stories.........and by interiorizing or exteriorizing oneself......which......is essentially the same thing," we can relive this story and thereby learn to understand and master the psychology of life.[22] Some people, she noted, have done precisely that; these are the ones considered as "initiates, occultists and prophets......." One contemporary individual who has done this in an in-depth and personally related way is C. G. Jung, with his essentially modern Gnostic creation myth and cosmology written in 1916, some four years after he began his active engagement with the unconscious.[23] He began consciously engaging the unconscious in 1912, elaborating his numinous fantasies in *The Red Book* with exquisite paintings, while engaging in written dialogues with different fantasy figures until 1930, at which time he stopped and earnestly took up the study of alchemy.[24]

JUNG'S INITIAL FANTASIES AND HIS SCIENTIFIC WORK

The importance of this period in the development of Jung's approach to psychology cannot be underestimated. Jung wrote:

---

[22] 2004, p.206.

[23] 2009, pp. 346-355 passim.

[24] C. G. Jung, 1965.

"The years...........when I pursued the inner images, were the most important time of my life. Everything else derived from this. It began at that time, and the later details hardly matter anymore. My entire life consisted in elaborating what had burst forth from the unconscious and flooded me like an enigmatic stream and threatened to break me. That was the stuff and material for more than only one life. Everything later was merely the outer classification, the scientific elaboration, and the integration into life. But the numinous beginning, which contained everything, was then.[25]"

He also noted that "it took me forty-five years to distill within the vessel of my scientific work the things I experienced and wrote down at the time.[26]" It is noteworthy that Jung gave greater importance to the initial inner experiences rather than the subsequent personal integration and elaboration of the material in his scientific work. Yet, it should not be undervalued that, although it all began with his early engagement with the unconscious, the complete material realization of his early discoveries took a lifetime of conscious work.

It is also significant that Jung felt that it was essential that he abandon the tendency to aesthetic elaboration for the sake of scientific understanding. The aesthetic attitude has the advantage of non-judgmental openness, but cannot deal with the shadow or evil, which requires ethical deliberation and judgment. He understood that such inner experiences come with an ethical obligation, which, in his case, meant the need to consciously embody and demonstrate to people in the external world the reality of the objective psyche, not only through his own experiences but others' as well.[27][28] Consequently, after his initial confrontation with the unconscious, the confrontational emphasis changed from the unconscious

---

[25] 2009, p. vii.

[26] Jung, 1965 p. 199.

[27] Jung 2009, pp. 218, 219.

[28] Jung 1965.

to the world, and he began giving many important lectures based on his own inner experiences as well as those of his clients.[29] Thus, both the foundation for the empirical study of the psyche and his education of others were established as a result of his overwhelming original experiences and dialogue with the unconscious.

SRI AUROBINDO'S, THE MOTHER'S AND JUNG'S CREATION STORIES

Jung had little access to primary source material on Gnosticism that is now available since the discoveries at Nag Hammadi in 1945 and the Dead Sea Scrolls between 1946 and 1956; and he had to rely on fragments of Gnostic material, as well as derogatory and distorted accounts of the Church Fathers, and their polemics against the Gnostics.[30] Nonetheless, his *Seven Sermons to the Dead* is, by and large, a Gnostic creation myth with contemporary relevance and a timeless message, a culminating mythological account of an important Western spiritual tradition.[31] In the Mother's explanation of a creation myth that she relates, it is a story that is "more or less complete, more or less expressive" that one relives[32]. Yet Jung's experiences went well beyond taking a traditional story and trying to relive it more or less well. His mythological story is rather a creation myth that acted as a culmination of some four years of intense inner visions and dreams, along with elaborate dialogues with fantasy figures and aesthetically pleasing paintings. These were Jung's subjective experiences of the objective and archetypal psyche that he was later able to consciously relate directly to his scientific work and relationship with the external world. After these experiences and his scientific elaboration, the reality of the psyche was, for Jung, an established fact.

In the Mother's creation story, which she warned her audience to not

---

[29] Jung, 2009, p. 219.
[30] Hoeller, 1994, p. 17.
[31] Ibid, p.32.
[32] 2004, p.206.

take as gospel, the Supreme exteriorized Himself in order to become self-aware, first as Knowledge-Consciousness and Force.[33] As, in the Supreme Will, there was an inherent instinct to express Joy and essential Freedom of being; four Beings were objectified to begin the developmental process of creation and the embodiment of these qualities. These Beings embodied the principles of Consciousness and Light, Life, Bliss and Love, and Truth. As soon as there was separation between the Supreme and His emanations through the Creative Force, immediately at the beginning of creation, Consciousness turned into inconscience, Light became darkness, Love turned into hatred, Bliss became suffering and Truth became falsehood. On witnessing this, the Creative Force turned to the Supreme and prayed for a remedy for the evil of creation. She was commanded by the Supreme to penetrate the inconscience with Her Consciousness, to infuse suffering with Love, and falsehood with Truth. Consequently, as the *Parashakti*, a greater Consciousness, a more total Love and a more perfect Truth than at the original act of creation plunged into the created universe in order to begin the process of redeeming the material creation and returning it to its Source.

In Sri Aurobindo's account of an important Vedic creation story, there were four kingly gods, four Luminous Beings, Varuna [Infinite Existence and Unity of Being], Mitra [Light of Consciousness, Love and Divine Harmony], Bhaga [Bliss and joy], and Aryaman [Power, Effective Will and Strength].[34] They were entrusted with creation by the Supermind, the creative Source of the manifestation, as fourfold Savitri, from whom they emanated. These four Beings were, in fact, later known as *Satchitananda*, Existence, Consciousness, Bliss, where Consciousness comes instinct with Force. Immediately upon separation from the Source and the act of creation the four Beings turned into their Shadow opposites. Sri Aurobindo described this original Fall in the following descriptive passage

---

[33] 2004.

[34] 1971.

from *Savitri*, where Being "plunged into the dark," which ultimately saves "Non-Being's night:[35]"

> *"In the passion and self-loss of the infinite/ When all was plunged in the negating void/................/ Invoking in world-time the timeless truth, /Bliss changed to sorrow, Knowledge made ignorant, /God's force turned into a child's helplessness/ Can bring down heaven by their sacrifice. / A contradiction founds the base of Life: The eternal, the divine Reality/ Has faced itself with its own contraries; / Being became the Void and Consciousness-Force/Nescience and a walk of a blind Energy/ And Ecstasy took the figure of world-pain.[36]"*

As with the Mother's creation story there was eventual redemption the possibility of which is suggested in the following passages in *Savitri*.

> *"At last the struggling Energy can emerge/ And meet the voiceless Being in wider fields; / Then can they see and speak and, breast to breast, / In a larger consciousness, a clearer light, / The Two embrace and strive and each know each/ Regarding closer now the playmate's face/........................../ In Nature he saw the mighty Spirit concealed, / Watched the weak birth of a Tremendous Force,......[37]"*

Sri Aurobindo's account of a Vedic creation myth and the Mother's story are relevant to this discussion as potential sources of comparison with Jung's account of the workings of the Primal Creative Shadow. The advent of redemption from the workings of the Shadow creation, in fact, ties Jung's creation myth, to which we will now turn, to these stories related by Sri Aurobindo and the Mother.

---

[35] 1970a, pp.140, 141.
[36] *Savitri: Book II, Canto IV, pp. 140, 141.*
[37] *Savitri: Book II, Canto IV, pp. 141.*

JUNG'S SEVEN SERMONS TO THE DEAD

Jung's title for his myth is *VII Sermones ad Mortuos* (*Seven Sermons to the Dead*), to which, according to the originally published tract, he attributed authorship to Basilides, the second century AD Gnostic who lived and taught in Alexandria.[38] In the source book itself, *The Red Book*, recently published for the first time, the main spokesman and author is Philemon, to whom Jung actually assigned all his early fantasy writings, including the *Seven Sermons to the Dead*.[39] Philemon, who came from Alexandria, was an archetypal wise old man and mercurial being, and a guru for Jung, to whom the latter attributed superior insight. According to *The Red Book*, he in fact, revealed himself as Simon Magus, perhaps the most important Father of Gnosticism.[40] The dead in the Gnostic tradition, and undoubtedly in Jung's view, are *hylic* individuals who identify with their physical and vital natures and deny their psychic and spiritual (pneumatic) beings. They are those who unreflectively and indiscriminately accept collective beliefs, including religious and spiritual dogma, doctrine and tradition. In the sermon, they are referred to as faithful Christians.

Attributing the *Seven Sermons to the Dead* to Philemon is significant for many reasons, many of which I discuss in another essay, *Jung, Philemon and the Fourfold Psyche*. For purposes of this essay, the fact that he carried four [4] keys is the most relevant fact, for four [4] is qualitatively an important number psychologically that symbolizes wholeness and completeness of individual being. Moreover, in the fourth Sermon, four [4] is "the number of the chief deities, because four [4] is the number of the measurements of the world.[41]" Thus, Philemon is related to the fundamental fourfold truth of existence and individual wholeness, and held the four [4] keys that open the doors to authentic self-knowledge.

---

[38] 1965.

[39] 2009.

[40] Ibid, p.359.

[41] Jung, 1965, p.385.

THE PLEROMA AND THE PRINCIPLE OF INDIVIDUATION

In the first Sermon, Philemon began by describing the Gnostic *Pleroma*, which is both emptiness and fullness, differentiated and undifferentiated, containing all the opposites in a state of equilibrium. In fact, the *Pleroma* has no qualities at all, given that the qualities attributed to the Pleroma are created by our thinking mind. But, authentic differentiation does not come from the intellect, but is derived from authentic being, and, therefore, the needful is to strive after one's true nature, not discrimination and differentiation through the intellect alone. The natural tendency of the incarnated soul, Philemon asserted, is to differentiate itself from the *Pleroma* and to learn true discrimination and discernment. Differentiation is the essence of the created world including man. The *principium individuationis*, the principle of individuation, involving the differentiation of being, is, in fact, a fundamental motive-force in Jung's approach to psychology.

According to Philemon, the *Pleroma* is described as completely pervading all existence of the created World, which includes being present to and permeating the individual human being. According to this Sermon, the created world, however, has no part in it, which is a way of saying that the *Pleroma* is veiled to human consciousness. Jung actually believed that the Self not only supports the world of duality like a reflective movie screen, a typical *Advaitan* metaphor, but that the essence of the Self is in the duality itself, particularly evident in archetypal experiences, where archetypes are "a priori structural forms of the stuff of consciousness.[42]" In fact, the danger confronting the individual, according to the first Sermon, is the seductive pull back into the abyss of the *Pleroma* in that it is nothingness and dissolution, while giving up the light of consciousness and the urge towards individuation. Here there is essential agreement with Sri Aurobindo and the Mother when the latter, commenting on some ideas presented by Sri Aurobindo, argues that a superior solution resides in the goal to seek a differentiated "Oneness which restores us to

---

[42] 1965, p. 347

the essential Delight of the manifestation and the becoming" rather than understanding the world to be based on desire with "total rejection of all desire and a return to annihilation.[43]" This was also Jung's goal and Philemon's message to the dead, the unregenerate psyche of the common person today, which will become clear below.

ABRAXAS, HELIOS AND THE DEVIL

God, says Philemon in the second Sermon, is the created world in as much as He is differentiated from the *Pleroma*. He is, as such, a quality of the *Pleroma*. Philemon then presents the reader with the differentiation of two significant polar opposites or contraries, *Helios*, on the one hand, God the Sun, the *summum bonum* [Supreme Good], representing fullness and generativity and *Eros* or relatedness, on the other hand, the Devil, the *infinum malum* (endless evil) representing emptiness, destruction, dissolution and *Thanatos* or death. In the manifest world, these two exist together as active opposites, each producing discernible effects.

There is yet another God that is differentiated from the *Pleroma*, yet its closest approximation. Human's do not perceive his power and he seems less effective than either *Helios* or the Devil. His name is *Abraxas*, and he transcends both the God *Helios* and the Devil and represents the power of reconciliation of all existential force and activity.

John I: 4 declares that: *All that came to be had life in him/and that life was the life of men, /a light that shines in the dark, /a light that darkness could not overpower.*[44] This description does not seem significantly different than the Vedic description of original Infinite light of Existence which had to come to terms with the darkness of the Non-Existence, which I discuss below. However, in the Vedic creation myth, recounted above, there is a development whereby, on creation and separation from the Source, the four Beings of light turn into their opposites, suggesting that the original Good and Light of Existence transcends the shadow creation, which

---

[43] 1957, p. 8.
[44] The Jerusalem Bible, 1966.

includes both inferior light and darkness. In the Christian story there is no such differentiation.

Jung, consequently, felt the need to spend a considerable amount of energy during the latter part of his life in trying to educate the Christian world on the shortcoming of its God as the *Summum Bonum*, All-Good, without a spot of darkness. According to Augustine and other Fathers of the Church, since God is All-Good and without blemish, then *omne bonum a Deo, omne malum ab homine*, all good from God, all evil from man, in other words man is the original source of evil, not God. Moreover, evil itself paradoxically has no reality and can only be *privatio boni*, the deprivation of good, without substance in its own right. Jung was particularly concerned that this doctrine encourages people not to take the shadow or evil seriously.

Jung was prepared to accept evil as *privatio boni* as a metaphysical truth, but in the duality of the manifest world, in a view similar to that expressed by Sri Aurobindo, he was adamant that there is a need to differentiate good and evil, each embodying an essential reality emanating from a superior Being. In this Gnostic myth, that Being is *Abraxas*, Himself, an unconscious shadow emanation in time of the non-dual *Pleroma*. Moreover, for Jung, the primary source of evil in the world and the author of human sins, like everything else, is logically, the paradoxical God. Such a view takes an excessive burden of sin off human shoulders, without discouraging the principal of individuation, with its own motive power, which necessitates the individual becoming conscious of different levels of the shadow. Sri Aurobindo and Jung both recognize evil as the consequence of separation from the creative Source, the Self or Brahman. Just as Jung acknowledges *privatio boni* as a metaphysical truth, the former grants evil the status of being a relative truth and of being "the creation of Ignorance and the unconscious," while "the adverse opposites," are specifically "creations of Life or Mind in Life" and, in the soul's journey of individuation, subject to discernment by the psychic being, the incarnated aspect of the soul.[45]

---

[45] Sri Aurobindo, 1970b, pp. 597, 606.

Abraxas is the supreme power of Being in whom light and darkness are each united and transcended. This power contains all the opposites of creation in a state of unconscious complementarities. Life is generated and regenerated through the power of *Abraxas*, a being which is impersonal, amoral, non-discriminating and merciless. This god is both the instinctual depths of the erect phallus of *Priapos*, and the archetypal heights of the spirit. *Abraxas* is the closest approximation to the active manifestation of the *Pleroma* consisting of force, endless time and continual change. As universal, undifferentiated psychic energy *Abraxas* generates both truth and falsehood, good and evil. It is the life of creation and illusory deceit, a power in the world of relative reality. Above all, counseled Philemon, this God is terrible, demanding fear [awe] and admiration.

ABRAXAS: PRIMORDIAL CREATIVE SHADOW PLEROMA

In the Gnostic tradition *Abraxas* is represented as a Rooster-headed god, with two powerful looking serpent legs, a whip in his right hand and a shield in his left, often depicted in a chariot drawn by four white horses at breakneck speed. The rooster head suggests conscious vigilance, the shield, protective "wisdom," the whip the "relentless, driving power of life," and the serpent legs, undifferentiated but powerful energy.[46] The four [4] white horses suggest that despite the undifferentiated energy comprising *Abraxas* and His essential play of Ignorance, there is not only wakeful witness, wisdom and the dynamic interplay of life, but the fourfold purified divine Force is drawing the Rooster-headed god forward. This view is supported by the fact that according to Sri Aurobindo, in the *Vedas*, while the cow symbolizes the Light of Consciousness, the horse symbolizes the dynamism of Force.[47]

Thus, *Abraxas* can be referred to as the primordial creative Shadow *Pleroma*, with a definite direct relationship to the Transcendent *Pleroma*, out of which *Abaxas* grows. Despite its fundamental unconsciousness

---

[46] Hoeller, 1994, p. 84.
[47] 1971.

and status as the essential Being of Ignorance, It is ultimately driven by a dynamic transcendent truth, however veiled to human consciousness. In fact, Jung's unknown God, *Abraxas*, manifests three important principles of Jungian psychology: [1] energy as libido: [2] the play of opposites, and: [3] the natural instinct towards individuation that demands gradually assimilating aspects of the unconscious *Abraxas* to consciousness and conscious differentiation. It implies the need to consciously come to terms with this undifferentiated energy through experiences of "conflicts of duty" with the power of moral discernment. This demands conscious access to what Jung refers to as the transcendent function, the reconciling third position beyond the opposites, based on experience of the Self, which goes beyond the answer given by dogmatic morality.

TRANSCENDING THE CONTRARIES OF LIFE

The depth, complexity and relevance of Jung's paradoxical manner of thinking and experiencing life, which fully engages what Sri Aurobindo refers to as the "*contradiction....[at] the base of life*" where, *the divine Reality/ Has faced itself with its own contraries,*" becomes increasingly evident as one penetrates further into his creation myth and its meaning.[48] In his own words, Jung observes that "The highest and the lowest, the best and the vilest, the truest and the most deceptive things are often blended together in the inner voice in the most baffling way, thus opening up in us an abyss of confusion, falsehood, and despair.[49]" Here Jung is speaking of being conscious of the experiential co-existence of a pair or more opposites, which requires more psychological maturity than the experience of one opposite after the other.

As Sri Aurobindo writes: "*All walks inarmed by its own opposites, / Error is the comrade of our mortal thought / And falsehood lurks in the deep bosom of truth, / Sin poisons with its vivid flowers of joy / Or leaves a red scar across the soul; / Virtue is a grey bondage and a goal. / At every step*

---

[48] 1970a.
[49] Jung, 1974, p. 185.

is laid for us a snare / Alien to reason and the spirit's light, / Our fount of action from a darkness well.[50] The resolution to the complex and confusing meeting of contraries comes by a creative synthesis in a third position, by appealing to the Self's transcendent function and the direct involvement of what Sri Aurobindo calls the psychic being, the incarnated soul. In other words, as Jung observes, the hero "discovers a new way" to fulfillment and wholeness of personality, and that "Personality is Tao.[51]" By engaging the opposites of life, writes Jung, the whole person "enters the fray with his total reality," allowing for the "creative confrontation with the opposites and the synthesis in the self," the wholeness of personality.....as the *coniunctio oppositorum.*[52] This eventually leads to a reconciliation between the opposites in the God-image itself, which is "the meaning of divine service ....so that light may emerge from darkness," consciousness from Ignorance. Conscious individuation takes one well beyond assimilation of the personal shadow to integration of one's relationship to the collective and archetypal Shadow, the Shadow side of the God-Image.[53]

Philemon has already introduced the reader to the two main oppositional forces in creation in *Helios*, God the Sun, as the highest good, and His opposite, the Devil, as endless evil. These two oppositional powers are reminiscent of the observation and principal concern of the ancient Vedic seers who see God as Varuna, the infinite light of existence, as the basis for perfection and the primary goal, but also recognize the obscure limitations imposed by "the dark Coverer, the adversary Vritra" who marred creation with his all-enveloping black shadow of an unformed Inconscience, as Non-Existence.[54] The subtle difference between the two conceptions is that, in the Vedic myth, the oppositional powers are conceived of as extensions of the One, whereas, in Jung's creation myth, they are extensions, not of the *Pleroma* per se, as the Transcendent One, but

---

[50] 1970a*, p. 440.

[51] 1970a*, p. 440.

[52] 1965, pp. 337.

[53] Ibid, p. 338.

[54] Sri Aurobindo, 1971, p. 448.

of *Abraxas*, the Shadow *Pleroma*. The embodiment of creative Ignorance, however, is an emanation of the transcendent *Pleroma*.

The Bhagavaad Gita describes a threefold Godhead that includes the transcendent Brahman, the *Purushottama*, and two subordinate positions, the *akṣara purusha*, the "soul in Brahman" and the *kṣara purusha*, the mutable "soul in Nature.[55]" The *akṣara purusha* is "the eternal silence" and witness soul, while, it's opposite the *kṣara purusha* is the Godhead in its "eternal activity.[56]" In each of these two subordinate positions, there are qualities found in the description of Abraxas both as vigilant wakefulness and eternally active energy. Noteworthy, however, is the fact that, according to the Gita, complete spiritual liberation, including involvement in life and the working of Nature, requires rising to the *Purushottama*, which is the supreme Master of works. This understanding is not found in Jung's metaphysics, although his transcendent function encourages going beyond the opposites at every turn in the play of life, and his approach to psychology requires full acceptance of life, the ever-present penetration of the Pleroma in life and the goal of consciousness-life. Relationship with the *Purushottama*, as Master of works, puts a spiritual emphasis on Jung's goal, which is consequently raised to a higher level.

THE FOUR PRINCIPAL DEITIES IN JUNG'S GNOSTIC CREATION MYTH

In Sermon four of the *Seven Sermons to the Dead* the reader learns that there are actually four [4] principal deities and that "four is the number of the measurements of the world.[57]" There are in addition to the two principal antagonists a great many goods and evils, a multiplicity of gods and devils, including two god-devils, the "Burning one," or *Eros*, and the "Growing one," or The Tree of Life and *Logos*. Along with *Helios* and the Devil, they comprise the four main gods of creation. As god-devils, *Eros*

---

[55] Sri Aurobindo, 1970c, pp. 175-296 passim, 279.

[56] Ibid.

[57] Jung, 1965, p. 385.

and *Logos* are not only opposites but they each contain within themselves oppositional powers of light and shadow. The mutual co-existence and interpenetration of these two powers of being contain the secret of the wholeness of personality.

The "Growing one" represents the spirit of civilization, the *Logos* of the *zeitgeist*. It continually creates institutions, regulations, codes of conduct, laws and ritual forms in order for life to expand on stable and secure ground. In Western Christianity, there is tradition, dogma and doctrine that can assist in one's religious growth, but it can also stultify, limit and encourage conformity. The totalitarian state is the worst offender against the individual spirit, although the "Growing One" functions repressively at all levels of culture, including in tribal societies, where social beliefs, rituals, and cyclic patterns of life can squelch the individual's drive for individuation. In addition to essential cultural expressions and the development of civilization, then, there is the shadow of rigid and inflexible conservatism and repression.

The "Burning one" or *Eros*, on the other hand, seeks life in creative change, the lure of adventure, risk, challenge and battle, although it can involve conflict and violence. *Eros* rebels against the restrictions of civilization as well as any ascetic life-negating quest for high-culture, knowledge and task and service specialization. *Eros* is also the horizontal impetus towards knowledge of and relationship with others. The "Burning One" thus represents the individual creative spirit and the impetus for individual truth, but also the shadowy wildness below the veneer of civilization and culture, both the joy and suffering of life.

In these four [4] gods can be seen the veiled workings of the *Pleroma*, known in Hindu mythology as *Sat Chit-Shakti Ananda* and *Asat*. Veiled behind the Sun God is pure Existence or *Sat* and behind the Devil is Non-Existence or *Asat*. Behind the "Growing One" as Tree of Life or *Logos* is Consciousness-Force or *Chit-Shakti* and behind "The Burning One" are Bliss and the joy of life, *Eros* as *Ananda*.

The relevance of these observations and the previous one about the Vedic god, Varuna and, and Shadow, Vritra, is that Jung's Gnostic creation myth is compatible with the creation stories related by Sri Aurobindo and

28

the Mother and referred to in my essay, *Jung, Philemon and the Fourfold Psyche*, although Jung's myth tends to place more emphasis on the created world of Ignorance itself, whereas the former two emphasize the act of creation and movement from the One to the manifest world of Ignorance and Inconscience. Perhaps this difference in perspective reflects Jung's vocation as a psychologist and the need to relate to people where they are, on the one hand, and Sri Aurobindo's and the Mother's more over-compassing mission as the *Avatar* and Divine Mother of our time - and the incarnation of the Supermind, the Truth mind. Jung's myth, in fact, is not only compatible but also complementary in that its focus adds psychological complexity and detail to the essential reality symbolically depicted in the two other stories recounted by the Mother and Sri Aurobindo. The same argument can be made in terms of Jung's approach to psychology in comparison to the psychological aspects of Integral Yoga as defined by Sri Aurobindo and the Mother.

THE DYNAMIC INTERPLAY BETWEEN LOGOS AND EROS: INTRAPSYCHIC AND INTERPSYCHIC

Jung's cosmology and myth continues to explore the paradoxical mystery behind the intuitive concepts of the two principles of *Logos*, the Word, and *Eros*, relatedness, and their embodiment and psychological interplay, especially between men and women. Following ancient tradition, Jung understood the feminine to be *Mater Coelestis*, the Heavenly Mother, who comes as a white dove, and the masculine to be *Phallos* the Earthly Father, manifesting as a serpent. The dove is ostensibly feminine and represents the spiritual power that both receives and comprehends, while the serpent represents the giving and generating male principle of procreation, which must receive in order to give.

In addition to *Logos,* the masculine principle possesses all the characteristics of *Eros* and the feminine principle, in addition to *Eros,* contains all the characteristics of *Logos. Logos* or meaning, governs the spiritual in men and the sexual and instinctual connectedness in women, while *Eros* or relatedness governs the spiritual in women and the sexual and instinctual in men. Thus, each gender is blessed with one *Logos* and one *Eros* principle but in an opposite manner. This is the basis for the mutual attraction and unconscious projections between men and women.

There is no better example of the conscious dynamic interplay of *Eros* and *Logos* than the energy flow between Sri Aurobindo and the Mother, the latter making manifest through her yoga Sri Aurobindo's essential qualities of the spirit of Logos, the Word, which, in fact, originally devolved through the Divine Mother. Even though the Mother assimilated Sri Aurobindo's qualities and could, for example, easily think in terms of ideas, by nature, she preferred to tell revealing stories and explain the latter's abstract formulations in practical terms that were understandable to her disciples and, at times, even to ashram children. Her yoga of the cells also made her conscious of her connectedness with all life at a cellular level, engendering a subtle influence throughout the physical manifestation.

On his part, Sri Aurobindo was also capable of making his views understandable to others, which he did especially in conversations and in his Letters on Yoga. Nolini Kanta Gupta is an excellent example of a male disciple who was able to stay true to his essentially male perspective and the *Logos* principle in his presentation of ideas, in particular as a conveyor of the Word according to Sri Aurobindo and the Mother and, at the same time, evidently having assimilated much of the *anima* or *Shakti*, in his simple, direct and meaningful well-articulated essays.

In the world of C. G. Jung, Jung's writings were generally relegated to the world of ideas involving the complex and paradoxical associations, which are often difficult to follow, although he has written some pieces in a more straight-forward and understandable humanly-related way, including many of his letters, his direct input to his autobiography and his essay in the book, *Man and his Symbols,* which he inspired and co-authored with some of his principal disciples. Jung's extraordinary ability to incarnate the spirit through feminine values is evident in the following observations: "The feeling for the infinite, he wrote....can be attained only if we are bounded to the utmost....in the experience I am only that! ....In such awareness, we experience ourselves concurrently as limited and eternal, as both one and the other. In knowing ourselves to be unique in our personal combination – that is, ultimately limited – we possess also the capacity for becoming conscious of the infinite. But only then![58]" Incarnation of spiritual truths and the embodied access to the infinite requires intimate relationship to the feminine and both her interconnectedness to all life and definitional limits.

Jung's female disciples, in particular, are responsible for having disseminated his work in a way that is understandable to the reading public. In my view, his most outstanding disciple is Marie Louise von Franz, who not only has a powerful connection to *Eros* in her life, but she had the capacity to intellectually translate Jung's works into meaningful and practical psychological understanding, especially in her psychological studies of Fairy Tales. She also wrote some books and essays, notably *Number and Time* and *Jung's Myth in Our Time,* where her own capacity for engaging in discourse involving complex ideas is very evident, indicating her assimilation of the male principle of *Logos* in her thinking. Edward Edinger is a first class example of a male disciple who is able to stay with his essentially male perspective and sense of meaning, and yet he clearly assimilated the *anima* to the point of allowing the principle of *Eros* to influence his writings, especially when he comments directly on some of Jung's more difficult works, by explaining Jung's ideas and adding practical considerations to bring them into psychological scrutiny and the conduct of every day life.

According to his natural pre-dispositions, the conscious male consequently naturally identifies with the mind, and law and order, which is directly connected to the feminine *Mater Coelestis*, the Goddess *Logos.* Since his spirituality "is more of heaven [and] it goeth to the greater" there is a tendency in a man's thinking, therefore, towards the realm of ideas, abstraction, and the spirit.[59] The principle of *Phallos* and the god *Eros*, meanwhile, tend to act upon the masculine nature from the unconscious, a reflection of the fact that a man's sexuality [and instinctuality] "is more of

---

[58] Ibid, p. 325.
[59] Ibid, p. 387.

the earth.[60]" Being consciously in touch with his sexuality and instinctual nature, therefore, keeps a man related and connected to earthly reality.

In contrast to the male psyche, where the Goddess *Logos* rules his conscious thinking, the great carrier of meaning for the female psyche is the god *Eros*, allowing women to be more related in their thinking, and meaningfully connected in relationship and instinctual and sexual relatedness. Her sexuality [and instinctual relatedness], accordingly, "is more of the spirit.[61]" Thus a woman is more likely to find meaning in sexuality and relationships than a man, where these dynamics of earthly life lay in the unconscious and are pretty well unconscious and blind.

For women, where the God *Eros* rules her conscious life, the Goddess *Logos,* on the other hand, acts from the unconscious. This allows the feminine psyche to function in the world, but without her perceiving meaning there as a man does. Despite the fact that her *Logos* functions unconsciously, she often does the right thing through woman's intuition thanks to her close relationship to the natural mind. Moreover, in contrast to men, where spirituality tends to move the mind towards ideas and the spirit, a woman's spirituality "is more of the earth.[62]" This means that a woman's thinking tends to be practical and down to earth, even when it turns to philosophy and psychology or yoga, or any other discipline requiring mental competence.

It becomes evident from this discussion that the dynamics of the psychic energy lying in the male psyche typically differs from those which lay in the female psyche. The requirements of individuation, which aims at wholeness, are therefore, quite different for men and for women, although the *principium individuationis,* the principle of individuation functions equally in either case. Wholeness implies integrating qualities of the opposite sex, in other words, androgyny, while, concomitantly, coming to terms with both spirituality and sexuality and the instinctual nature. Spirituality and sexuality [and the instinctual nature] are manifestations of the gods, one could say,

---

[60] ibid, p. 387.
[61] Ibid, p. 387.
[62] Ibid, p. 387.

the other side of the coin, and exist objectively in their own right. Thus, the individuating psyche must learn to detach itself from these archetypal daimons, yet not repress them, as the psyche is subject to their laws.

Men and women must become conscious of both the god *Eros* and the goddess *Logos* that lay in their respective unconscious, or else remain victimized by them. In psychological terms, there is a need, in other words, for men to become conscious of, first their personal shadow, and then their *anima*, the feminine mediatrix and bridge to the deeper unconscious in men. There is, likewise, a need for women to become conscious of their personal shadow and then the *animus*, the masculine beacon and bridge to the collective unconscious in women. In the measure that this is not done, one is possessed by unconscious complexes, typically meaning that the shadow opposite of one's conscious ego and expressed persona exists albeit unconsciously. The self-styled benign leader, for instance, deliberately acts according to conscious notions of doing good service, while potentially being driven by a Mephistophelean power drive. The well-meaning husband or wife communicates reasonably with their spouse based on the principles of communication skills for couples, and yet there may have been no conscious resolution of underlying anger, power drive and victim complexes, which continues to haunt the relationship.

Humankind requires both life in community as well as solitude, each ideally in harmony with both *Logos* and *Eros*. Community gives "warmth" and "depth", while solitude gives "light" and "height," observes Philemon.[63] From a psychological perspective, community serves the purpose of generating human warmth and depth through relationships and work in the community, while solitude engenders the light of consciousness and spiritual elevation. Jung reversed the normal view of life as he states that community requires abstinence, while solitude, through such activities as active imagination and the direct engagement of the multiple psyche requires the expression of abundance, "prodigality.[64]" In addition to the proper attitude towards both solitude and community,

---

[63] Ibid, p. 388.
[64] ibid, p. 388.

the consciously individuating psyche needs to find a judicious balance between the two. Too much or too little of either is evil, which is to say psychologically unhealthy, while the right measure, "as much communion as is needful," purifies.[65] Jung's insights expressed here on the nature of intra-psychic dynamics and both the interplay between men and women and community and solitude are invaluable to the contemporary seeker for community in a New World.

TWO OF JUNG'S INITIATION DREAMS: CHILDHOOD AND MIDLIFE

When Jung was somewhere between three and four years old he had an impressive dream where he climbs down a square opening in a meadow, to find himself, after pushing aside a sumptuous green curtain, in a well-appointed underground temple with a blood-red carpet on a flagstone floor that ends at a platform. The central focus of the dream is the platform with a rich golden throne upon which stands a roughly one and a half foot thick, twelve to fifteen foot high phallus. The head of the phallus, above which is "an aura of brightness," has a single eye that gazes motionlessly upward.[66]

In terms of amplification, the Hindu tradition of Shiva's *Lingam*, the sacred universal masculine generative spirit contained in the *Yoni*, the feminine universal womb, is particularly relevant. In Jung's dream, the masculine phallus is, likewise, standing on a rich golden throne, the Mother's seat as royal container. The head of the phallus has an aura of brightness and the eye gazes steadily upward, suggesting an incarnated divinity, whose intrinsic intent is continual aspiration and vertical relatedness to a superior entity. In the Hindu system, there are incarnated *purushas* at different levels of being, including the physical, each of which is supported by the psychic being, the *caitya purusha*, the incarnated aspect of the soul, and a direct delegation from the *Jivatman*, the individual soul, itself an aspect of the universal and transcendent *Atmans*.

Jung believed that he was initiated here into "the mystery of Earth,"

---

[65] Ibid, p. 388.
[66] Ibid, p. 12.

with her covering of green vegetation.[67] He was made aware of the Hidden God, "not to be named," a compensatory corrective to an overly self-conscious orientation to the Good and soulless Christianity, which represses the truths of the instinctual and earthly.[68] The square shape of the opening has the same symbolic significance as the earth. In alchemy the earth is a *coagulatio* operation, which means that it allows psychic experiences to be related to ego consciousness. Sri Aurobindo observed that the square is a symbol for the Supermind or Truth-mind, suggesting conscious relationship with the humble earth supports a relationship with the truth of being. The psychological unfolding of Jung's personal life and the development of his depth psychology both give rich evidence for his having assimilated the message behind this numinous experience. The important role given to the symbolic serpent in *The Seven Sermons to the Dead* gives further corroborating evidence.

Around Christmas 1912, when he was 37 years old and at the beginning of the time he refers to as his "confrontation with the unconscious," not knowing what myth he was living, while honestly acknowledging that it was not the Christian myth, he had another initiatory dream of great importance.[69] In the dream:

> *Jung finds himself in a magnificent Italian loggia situated high up on a castle tower. He is sitting on a gold Renaissance chair at a table of exquisite beauty made of emerald colored stone. He was looking out into the distance when a white dove or gull descends and lands on the table. The dove is immediately transformed into a little girl about eight years old with golden blonde hair. She runs off to play with Jung's children, who are also there, eventually returning and tenderly placing her arm around his neck. She suddenly vanishes as the dove re-appears and slowly says: "Only in the*

---

[67] Ibid, p.13.

[68] Ibid, p. 13.

[69] Ibid, p. 171.

first hours of the night can I transform myself into a human being, while the male dove is busy with the twelve dead.[70]"

The most significant reference for amplification of this dream is the descent of the dove during Jesus' baptism by John the Baptist, initiating Jesus' ministry as the anointed Son of the Father. The dove in the mainline Christian tradition symbolizes the Holy Ghost and is usually depicted as masculine. In the Gnostic tradition it is often viewed as feminine and the embodiment of Sophia, the carrier of the Word and divine wisdom. According to alchemical tradition, the legendary Hermes Trismegistos left behind an emerald table, where the tenets of essential alchemical wisdom were engraved in Greek. That the dove becomes an eight [8] year old girl who plays with Jung's children suggests that Jung's new potential relate playfully with a youthful embodiment of wisdom. The fact that the female dove becomes human and lands on the emerald table suggests that Jung can now potentially relate to psychological life situations with alchemical wisdom, not just with abstract intellectual concepts.

The enigmatic statement that the male dove is occupied with the twelve dead during the early hours of the night, allowing the female dove to become human, seems to suggest that when wisdom is humanized, twelve presently dead or repressed aspects of the psyche are being penetrated with the spirit of truth, the male dove. As far as the dead are concerned, they are presently repressed and unconscious, but potentially alive and conscious aspects of the psyche with the application of *Tapas* or the concentration of energy-Force. Qualitatively the number twelve [12] refers to cosmic harmony, as suggested by the twelve [12] signs of the zodiac, the twelve [12] Disciples of Christ, and the twelve [12] petals around the Matrimandir (Sanskrit: Temple of The Mother), which, according to the Mother, represent twelve [12] qualities of the universal Mother.[71]

The symbolism of the dream indicates that Jung was being directly initiated by *Mater Coelestis*, the Heavenly Mother, with the Word for a life

---

[70] Ibid, pp. 171, 172.
[71] The Mother (La Mère), 1982.

of embodied wisdom that includes a conscious relationship to universal or cosmic harmony. The wisdom he gained is the wisdom of alchemical transformation, which does not just involve the individual and personal world of the microcosm, but is intimately related to the macrocosm and to the transformation of the collective. Jung actually began serious study of alchemy in 1926, at the end of his experiment with the unconscious, and alchemy became, along with Gnosticism, the major hermeneutic and interpretive lens for his approach to psychology from then on. Significantly, in alchemy, there is complete acceptance of the earthly feminine and concretization of the spirit or incarnation of the Divine Will, which one does not find in Gnosticism.

These reflections on Jung's two dreams take one to further psychological considerations on the relevance of the serpent and the dove symbolism. In harmony with the complex interplay of opposites at all levels of being, according to the meaning Jung attributes to the serpent, it is outwardly masculine and phallic, but inwardly feminine and enkindles or is receptive to desire. In a similar way, the dove is outwardly feminine, but inwardly masculine and represents conscious thought and messages from the spirit and transcendence. The serpent and the dove, therefore, each make up half the human psyche of which one must become conscious for the sake of *Gnosis* or spiritual Knowledge. Although it is normally accepted that messages of transcendence and the spirit can be helpful to leading a meaningful spiritual life, it is not so well understood that acceptance of one's instinctual force and desire nature is also a *sine qua non* for coming in touch with one's spiritual wholeness.

THE PATH OF INDIVIDUATION

Following the way of the serpent does not mean to do so blindly or unconsciously and without discipline, which would only lead to further unconsciousness. In the language of Indian psychology it would involve becoming further enmeshed in the *kleshas* of existence. But it does mean that there is a need to consciously follow the instinctual

37

forces of desire, even, to allow oneself to be lead by them. This inevitably involves conflict and the need to experience and hold in consciousness a tension of opposites, including at times apparent chaos, in order to gain consciousness of *Eros* or relatedness and the heart Self or psychic being. Like Goethe's Mephistopheles, the serpent shows us the way in a manner that one would never chose by one's own conscious will. In Gnosticism, the serpent is regarded as both wild beast and holy counselor, the symbol of supernal wisdom. Not repression, but loving regard for one's nature, consciousness of one's desires and creative imagination connect one to the serpentine path of Self-Knowledge.

There is a need not to take change, which is a movement of nature *per se*, for psychological and spiritual transformation, which requires the *opus contra naturam*, the alchemical work of transformation against nature. In the alchemical view, individuals are the unique link between the microcosm, which includes their personal experiences and the world inside themselves, and the macrocosm, the world of the transcendental cosmic being, and the world outside themselves. One encounters here two aspects of the mystery of Existence that meet in the human psyche and, consequently, relate directly to what Jung refers to as synchronicity or the meaningful coincidence of outer and inner events. Jung understands synchronicity to involve observable non-dual experiences of general acausal orderedness, which implies that the manifestation is nothing less than the unfolding of a superior divine Will, the divine *Shakti* as manifestation of the *Purusha*. At times, one experiences this reality through archetypal experiences and synchronicity, as light penetrates the darkness of the Shadow existence.

According to Philemon, individuals have the task of following their own inner star, which are their differentiated *Pleroma* and God, and the goal of individuation. The implication of this statement is that God or the God-Image is an existential reality that can be experienced in one's individual psyche. Indeed, individuals need to attend to increasing the light of this star, which is to say become more conscious of the God-Image in their own soul through *Tapas*, or *askesis* and the application of effective will. As Jung argues throughout his writings, not only does man need

God but God also needs man in order to fulfill His purpose and to effect His transformation. Engaging the power of imagination through dynamic meditation approaches such as Jung's Active Imagination as depicted in *The Red Book* can allow one to become more aware of the indwelling Godhead and Its realization in life.

Humans can be turned away from their own God and conscious engagement in the individuation process by influence of the fiery outpouring of *Abraxas*, which is to say by the naturalistic psyche of worldliness, gross materialism, sensuality and even false optimism and idealism, among other things. The great danger to spiritually inclined people, however, is that they can too easily sacrifice *Abraxas* or life to the star, through spiritual ambition. Humankind is placed between life and spiritual reality and one should not identify with either. The *principium individuationis* always insists on the continual refinement and differentiation of individual consciousness, and not on dissolution of being in the *Pleroma* or non-differentiation of being swallowed up by *Abraxas*. Moreover, individuation has nothing to do with ego individualism or individualism with social interest as they are normally understood, but differentiation of collective aspects of the individual psyche through the Self. It involves forging a unique and homogeneous identity. Life in the material world is indispensable to spirit, for spiritual truths alone are irrelevant, Jung believes, if they cannot be incarnated in life. Consciousness is not enough; individuation refers to consciousness-life.

DETACHMENT AND INVOLVEMENT: PSYCHIC TRANSFORMATION AND SPIRITUAL ASCENSION

The path of individuation requires first psychological detachment and then full involvement in life. A period of detachment allows one to re-enter life with superior consciousness and ability to assimilate new material to consciousness without losing one's ground. First there is a need to separate from *Abraxas* for the sake of becoming a separate individual. Then, the task for the separate individual is to consciously unite with the subtle *Abraxas,* which is done by relating to one's soul [anima/animus] and forging a bridge to what Jung refers to as the Tree of Seven Lights. This tree grows out of the head of *Abraxas,* which in turn, grows from the *Pleroma.* Noteworthy is the fact that, in Jung's cosmology, the Tree of Life differs from the Tree of Light in that the former refers to civilization as a play of *Abraxas,* which always has a repressive side, sometimes more sometimes less, whereas the latter points to the light of consciousness and archetypal patterns behind life.

In Jung's Gnostic formulation, the first light is the *Pleroma,* the second, *Abraxas,* the third the sun, the fourth the moon, the fifth the earth, the sixth, the phallus, and the seventh, the stars. Each of these images needs to be understood symbolically. The seventh light is, in fact, an egg-golden bird or slumbering God that, when awake, leads individuals to their star, their personal portal to the *Pleroma.* Connection to the *Pleroma* and the single star, the one God, for which there is a need to increase its light by prayer or *Tapas,* the concentration of energy and application of effective will, comes by way of relatedness to *Mater Coelestis,* the Heavenly Mother [and the sky and birds].

Once one consciously unites with the subtle *Abraxas, Agni,* the Vedic inner flame and sacrificial fire, or *Phanes,* the Orphic creator god, is released from the form of the egg-golden bird or slumbering God to become a golden bird, which leads the individual upwards to the star through the Heavenly Mother. In Sri Aurobindo's symbolic system, *Agni* refers to "the psychic fire of aspiration, purification and Tapasya.[72]" Thus, as golden bird, the flame of aspiration released from the Tree of Seven Lights mounts vertically by way of sacrifice, purification and spiritual aspiration.

The flame is one and symbolizes unity, whereas the other six lights form a multiplicity, all situated on the Tree of Light. Since the one gives rise to the many and the many devolve to the one, the Tree of Light itself seems to foreshadow what Jung later defines as *unus mundus,* one world involving both unity and multiplicity and can be taken as an eighth factor

---

[72] 1966, p. 5.

in his archetypal image of manifest being. Aspiration to the single star or One God, and differentiated *Pleroma*, it should be noted, involves a highly individuated and conscious individual according to the *principium individuationis*, which runs as a leitmotiv throughout the *Seven Sermons to the Dead*. Although Jung makes no such reference, in my estimation, the emphasis on individuation and consciousness as well as aspiration to the *Pleroma* opens up the possibility of experiencing *samadhishta*, a self-gathered and waking state of *Samadhi*, along with its full realization in a globalized life, a theme which I discuss in *Jung's Global Vision Western Psyche Eastern Mind*.

Here, it is interesting to note that Sri Aurobindo also differentiated a sevenfold cord of being, the mental, the vital and the physical, along with the One as the triple *Sat Chit Ananda* and the link mind, the Supermind, the spiritual fourth, along with an eighth cord, the individual psychic being. The psychic being is the incarnated aspect of the soul involved in life that naturally aspires towards Truth, which it knows through feeling. The Supermind or Truth-mind links the multiplicity of the mental, vital and physical creation with the unitary spiritual reality of *Sat Chit Ananda*. Although Sri Aurobindo's cords of being are more clearly defined and not identical with Jung's formulation of the Tree of Light, there are essential similarities, including the flame of spiritual aspiration and the factor unifying unity and multiplicity.

One can, in any case, ascertain a similar archetypal pattern and order in each case with the need to consciously relate to unity in multiplicity by increasing the light of the star and incarnating the spirit in life in Jung's case, and in incarnating the Supermind in the case of Sri Aurobindo. With Jung there seems to be emphasis placed on becoming conscious of the archetypal patterns behind the Shadow creation itself which necessitates involvement of the soul and the psychic transformation in Sri Aurobindo and the Mother's terminology, and then spiritual transformation, involving vertical aspiration towards the one star, through intense relatedness with the Heavenly or Divine Mother. In terms of Vedic symbolism this is the work of Aryaman, with his aspiration and application of effective will and strength through *Tapas*. In comparison to Jung with the unifying function of the Tree of Light in his cosmology, and psychic and spiritual transformations, Sri Aurobindo's symbol system goes further, putting emphasis on the triple transformation, psychic, spiritual and supramental, involving relationship with *Sat Chit Ananda* as well as with a relatively well-defined Supermind and its unifying principle of creative ordering.

Later, Jung comes closer to Sri Aurobindo's articulation with his *unus mundus*, and three stages of conjunction based on the alchemical writings of Gerhard Dorn. They include the *unio mentalis*, union of unio mentalis with the world, and union of the individual *Atman* with the cosmic *Atman* and the individual Tao with the universal Tao for realization of the *unus mundus*.

****

True Gnosis involves Knowledge of the heart and not the head or ego. This is the real goal of individuation and Jung's Gnostic psychology. A supreme example of this Gnosis is Jung himself, who managed to assimilate to consciousness a considerable amount of the fullness of the *Pleroma* and its Shadow creation, while communicating to the world a path of Knowledge that includes a full life in the broad sense of the word and its psychic, or heart-Self centered transformation and spiritual transfiguration. An examination of the two dreams reported above provides ample evidence for the former assertion and his later visions, which I discuss in an essay on *Jung's Later Visions, Individualized Global consciousness and Completed individuation*, for the latter. Some of Jung's major disciples see him as a Prophet in the old Hebrew sense of the word, where Prophet means one who speaks with divine inspiration. Given his outstanding achievement in the development of a complex and detailed integral psychology, his *mana* personality, his remarkable inner experiences, and the fact that his life and work are one, in Hindu nomenclature, Jung would also certainly be identified as a *Vibhuti*, where *Vibhuti* refers to the manifest power of God. If Sri Aurobindo and the Mother are the *Avatars* and *Vibhutis* of the Supermind, then Jung was a Prophet and *Vibhuti* for the currently incarnating Deity, the living God.

REFERENCES

Sri Aurobindo (1966). Dictionary of sri aurobindo's yoga. Pondicherry: Dipti Publications, Sri Aurobindo Ashram.

Sri Aurobindo (1970a). Sri Aurobindo Birth Centenary Library. Popular Edition. Savitri: A legend and a symbol: Part one. Volume 28. Pondicherry: Sri Aurobindo Ashram

Sri Aurobindo (1970a*). Sri Aurobindo Birth Centenary Library. Popular Edition. Savitri: A legend and a symbol: Part two and three. Volume 29. Pondicherry: Sri Aurobindo Ashram.

Sri Aurobindo (1970b). Sri Aurobindo Birth Centenary Library. Popular Edition. The life divine: Book two part one. Volume 18. Pondicherry: Sri Aurobindo Ashram.

Sri Aurobindo (1970c). Sri Aurobindo Birth Centenary Library. Popular Edition. Essays on the gita. Volume 13. Pondicherry: Sri Aurobindo Ashram.

Sri Aurobindo (1971). Sri Aurobindo Birth Centenary Library. Popular Edition. The secret of the veda. Volume 10. Pondicherry: Sri Aurobindo Ashram.

The Mother (2004). Collected Works of the Mother. Questions and answers: 1957-58. Volume 9. Originally published in 1977. Second Edition. Pondicherry: Sri Aurobindo Ashram Publication Department.

The Mother (La Mère) (1982). L'agenda de mère: Volume XIII: 1972 – 1973: Agenda de L'action supramentale sur la terre. Paris: Institut de Recherches Évolutives.

Stephan A. Hoeller (1994). The gnostic jung and the seven sermons to the dead. Wheaton Ill. The Theosophical Publishing House.

John 1:4. The jerusalem bible. New York: Doubleday & Company, Inc.

C. G. Jung (2009). Philemon Series. The red book: Liber novus. Sonu Shamsdasani, editor. Preface by Ulrich Hoerni. Translated by Mark Kyburz, John Peck, and Sonu Shamdasani. New York: W. W. Norton & Company.

C. G. Jung (1965). Memories, dreams, reflections. Recorded and edited by Aniela Jaffé. Translated from the German by Richard and Clara Winston. Revised Edition. New York: Random House Inc.

C. G. Jung (1974). Collected Works. *The development* of personality. In The development of personality. Volume 17. Translated by R. F. C. Hull. Princeton NJ: Princeton University Press.

J. R.R. TOLKIEN'S PROPHETIC VOICE AND THE MYTHICAL PSYCHE: WITH REFERENCE TO C. G. JUNG

David Johnston

ABSTRACT

In this essay, I discuss the meaning of J. R.R. Tolkien's mythology, especially as portrayed in *The Lord of the Rings*. I also make comparative references to the work of C. G. Jung, with which I find compelling compatibility. I argue that the former brings the necessary compensatory vision to our contemporary culture and times in a way that is in harmony with the latter's perspective and concerns. As an artist, Tolkien was able to penetrate to the core of our Western cultural dynamics, and his sub-creation gives us images, words, language, values and a view that can serve as a light that illuminates our deeper needs for collective individuation and the way towards the future. Like a shaman, Tolkien made extended journeys throughout the archetypal worlds of Faërie and reported back what he experienced to the community at large. His message involves the requirement to assimilate both pagan sensibility and Christian values to consciousness, each of which have slipped into the unconscious in our one-sided scientific and technological, consumer-driven world. Tolkien has also given us imagistic and feeling examples of the path of individuation as articulated by Jung and the forces with which one has to contend. Giving up the Ring of Power and living more according to Eros and feeling values, both as individuals and as a culture, is essential. My personal belief is that Tolkien was a genius and prophet for our times, and we would do well to pay heed to his message and its meaning.

J.R.R. TOLKIEN'S PROPHETIC VOICE AND THE MYTHICAL PSYCHE: WITH REFERENCE TO C. G. JUNG

INTRODUCTION

I recently read *The Lord of the Rings* again after many years, this time after long involvement in a Jungian way of understanding and living life. I also read several other books about Tolkien and his legendarium as well as both *The Hobbit* and *The Silmarillion*. Initially published in 1937, *The Hobbit* was Tolkien's first published fantasy book and, in some ways, it can be understood as a precursor to *The Lord of the Rings*.[73] Tolkien wrote *The Silmarillion* for over half a century, the earliest versions of the main stories extending back to 1917, and continued to work on it until the end of his life.[74] Tolkien conceived of it as a compilation from various sources of poems, annals and oral tales that have survived from an age-long tradition. They recount the history of the world from its initial creation throughout the first three Ages of Man to the end of the Third Age and the departure of Frodo, Bilbo, the two Ring-bearers and others. They also delineate the essential mythological background material for both *The Hobbit* and *The Lord of the Rings*, which is especially relevant in the latter. Although Tolkien would have preferred that *The Silmarillion* were published in 'conjunction or connection' with *The Lord of the Rings*, the third and final volume of which entered the marketplace in 1955, it wasn't published until four years after his death, in 1977.[75]

---

[73] J. R. R. Tolkien, 1999a.

[74] 1999b.

[75] Ibid, p. viii, 2005c

Tolkien's sub-created world is subtle, complex, nuanced and layered; his work is written with both high erudition and the interrelatedness of Eros, with feeling, intuitive insight, realistic consistency and a sense of meaning. I am astonished at the parallels between Tolkien's works and Jung's and, especially, at the sense of wholeness and the intricacies regarding the individuation process that permeates *The Lord of the Rings* in particular and Tolkien's legendarium in general. This would not be possible had the work been contrived.

THE LORD OF THE RINGS IN BRIEF

In brief, the drama of *The Lord of the Rings* involves a quest by Frodo the Hobbit to give up the Ring of Power, a task entrusted to him by the wizard, Gandalf the Grey. He is joined at the outset by his faithful servant, Sam, and then two younger hobbits, Merry and Pippin. Hobbits are humans of a sort, standing some two to four feet tall, and known by men as Halflings, the Little Folk and the Little People.[76] Not only was the quest initiated by Gandalf, but he seems to always be involved in the organization of events, even when he was not present. He chose Frodo to be the Ring-bearer because of the humility and courage in the face of terror of Hobbits in general and Frodo in particular, who also had the advantage of being close to the previous Ring-bearer, Bilbo. He was also impressed with Frodo's adventuresome spirit.

The epic consists of several related stories including the struggles and burden of Strider, the future King as Aragorn (Elf-Sindarin: 'royal tree'), son of Arathorn (Elf-Sindarin: 'royal-') his crowning and marriage with Arwen (Sindarin: 'royal maiden'), the beautiful Elf-Maiden; it includes the destruction and renewal of the Shire thanks to the love of Sam, Frodo's loyal servant. It also includes Hobbits, Men and Dwarves forging a relationship with Elves, especially through the Elf-Queen, Galadriel (Elf-Sindarin: 'lady of light'), and her gifts of renewal. Finally, it involves the

---

[76] Robert Foster, 1978

transfiguration of the Istari (Elf-Quenya), Gandalf the Grey to Gandalf the White after his death embracing struggle with the terror-inducing Balrog (Elf-Sindarin: 'power-terror' or 'demon of might'), a rebellious Maiar and servant of Melkor (Elf-Quenya: 'He who rises in might'), the most knowledgeable and mightiest of the powers of the One and fallen Angel.[77] To see Gandalf in a wider perspective, the Istari, who were probably Maiar (Elf-Quenya), were charged with the specific task of counseling and uniting the Free People in their struggles against Evil. In fact, Aragorn acknowledges Gandalf as the "mover of all that has been accomplished, and this is his victory.[78]" The Maiar were lesser powers of the One who entered the Creation in order to tend the Earth under the direction of the Valar (Elf-Quenya: 'angelic powers'), the greatest powers of the Illúvatar (Quenya: 'all-father'), the One. [79]

During the quest, Frodo and the three other hobbits, found solace in their meeting with Tom Bombadil, the Original Man, and his spouse, Goldberry, entering their natural paradisiacal world of pure and unadulterated goodness, related to the beginning of time prior to the Fall. Always singing, Bombadil continually expresses light and melody from the original Light and Music of Creation, and Goldberry, the River-woman's daughter, is the symbolic embodiment of the ever-flowing river of unfolding life, the primal Feminine. The Ents or tree herds and guardians of the olvar (Quenya: 'growing things with roots in the ground'), which are awakened and self-aware mobile trees, were also enlisted in the Ring quest. Finally, the epic involved an enormous and dangerous struggle against Sauron (Elf-Quenya: 'abominable'), the rebellious Maiar and Shadow of Mordor (Elf- Sindarin: 'black land'), and all the other evil forces, Nazgûl (Black Speech: *nazg* 'ring' + *gûl* race), Orcs, Uruk-Hai (Black Speech: Orc-race), the Barrow-Wights, evil spirits of Angmar (Elf-Sindarin: 'iron-home') and the two Istari traitors, Sauruman and the terrible Balrog, that were trying to dominate

---

[77] Ibid
[78] Tolkien 2005c, p. 1004.
[79] Ibid

Middle-earth. Middle-earth consists of certain delineated parts of Arda [Elf-Quenya: region, realm], the Earth, especially related to Europe. Psychologically, the story is about a struggle for consciousness of the destructive shadow and the surrender of the Ring of Power and ambition for dominion over others. It is, more deeply, an epic concerned with the twin themes of death and immortality.

THE PROPHETIC VOICES OF C. G. JUNG AND J. R. R. TOLKIEN

There are genuine prophetic voices and indications today that exist in precisely the same way as they existed in the time of the prophets in Jewish history and elsewhere at all times. Foremost amongst them are the voices of C. G. Jung and J. R. R. Tolkien. As has always been the case regarding prophetic inspirations, there is considerable resistance to their messages, which are effectively identical at least inasmuch as deep social change depends on the far-reaching process of individuation of selected individuals. In the contemporary world, this resistance is largely due to the highly organized nature of life and the misplaced belief in the primacy of conscious intent and will. As is ever the case, we need to understand the prophetic voices and pay heed to their message. I say this, realizing that most people today do not believe that there is such a thing as a true prophet and certainly not one that relates to the life of our times.

The basic prophetic message in our time, as in the past, is that there is a need for renewal, which happens by way of individuals and society connecting, both in ideals and dynamic living, with the evolving archetypal substratum of the psyche. The archetypal psyche is the region where one can forge a relationship with the fundamental ways of apprehending life and life's basic patterns, which exist behind everyday life as we know and experience it. In other words, we need to relate directly to the manifest god, which in Judeo-Christian terms refers to a renewed and conscious covenant with a transcendent God, who is in harmony with the deeper demands of the times. In order to gain some understanding of what that refers to today, I will briefly allude to the work of C. G.

Jung, the psychologist, and J. R. R. Tolkien, especially in reference to his masterpiece, *The Lord of the Rings.*

The number four [4] is a fundamental leitmotif running throughout *The Lord of the Rings,* suggesting that it is the fundamental structural ground and deeper foundational reality of the epic. I will go into this subject later when I talk more specifically about Tolkien and *The Lord of the Rings.* Suffice it to say, at the moment, qualitatively, the number four [4] relates to wholeness and completion and the incarnated Self. In Jung's view it is a very important number and a symbol for individuation and wholeness of being. In the West and in the contemporary scientific world we think more quantitatively, which has its on validity, but, as I go along, I will appeal to you to make a shift of perception to see numbers qualitatively and not merely as a measure of quantity. So, for instance, when the number four [4] is constellated in the psyche through a dream or true fantasy; that means that a compensatory wholeness is potentially emerging into consciousness in order to bring harmony and balance to a relatively one-sided way of being.

JUNG, THE INDIVIDUATION PROCESS AND THE INDIVIDUATION OF HUMANKIND

Jung scientifically observed the spontaneous activity of the unconscious happening over and over again, having the same salutary effect when the contents were assimilated to consciousness. The goal of his approach to therapy is individuation and the individuation process, which means finding and becoming conscious of one's unique path to wholeness. Fundamentally, this refers to two factors; developing a personal relationship to the archetypal psyche, especially the central archetype, the Self, and the increasing differentiation of one's nature.

The archetypes refer to the way we apprehend the world and dynamically live in the world. They are the fundamental blueprints for action and the instinct's self-perception. Individuals living in harmony with the archetypes are living in instinctual harmony, which, when one is involved in the individuation process can become conscious. Individual's living consciously in relationship with the archetype of the Self, the centre of the psyche, live in relationship with their wholeness and have a connection to the infinite.

In practical terms, individuation of one's nature refers to the instinctive drive to differentiate all four functions of consciousness, thinking, feeling, sensation and intuition as well as the two attitudes, introversion and extraversion. In *The Lord of the Rings*, this is embodied in the four hobbits that go on the heroic quest. It can also be understood as the individualization of one's soul-type as priest, leader, trader and servant, which requires some differentiation of all qualities of being, all functions of consciousness and attitudes. In the epic, these specific soul-types are primarily embodied in Gandalf the wizard, Aragorn the King, Frodo, the bourgeois [trader] and his servant Sam. I will discuss these examples of individuation in more detail later.

At this point I will simply observe that the one-sidedness of our culture, which is driven by science and technology and consumer-oriented marketing, needs to become open to the assimilation and containment of the archetypal forces that are presently trying to emerge into our conscious reality. These archetypes are, in fact, great formative powers that seek realization, powers that can no longer abide staying in the ethereal air of idealism. I am speaking here not only of individuals but of the culture in general.

According to mythical accounts, the final stage of the heroic journey requires individual heroes to bring the boon or treasure back home so that others and the community can profit by it. In the case of Jung, he found vehicles to communicate his findings in alchemy and Gnosticism, allowing him to explain his experiences in a way that is understandable to individuals on the path of conscious individuation. Near the end of his life, despite some resistance and with the help of Aniela Jaffé, he also wrote an autobiography entitled *Memories, Dreams, Reflections* that has influenced countless numbers of average people[80]. Moreover, based on a

---

[80] C. G. Jung, 1965

dream, where he found himself on a hill delivering his message to ordinary folk, who *understood* what he was saying, he also wrote a piece for a book, which he organized and edited, called *Man and his Symbols.*

Jung's opus is principally concerned with the individuation of individuals, although it also refers to the individuation of culture, especially Western Culture. That both levels of the psyche are addressed by his work is possible because, at the archetypal level, the microcosm and the macrocosm are one. In fact, he often directly addressed the needs of Western culture and the modern mind. A citation honoring Jung at the Federal Technical Institute in Zurich, where he taught for several years, referred to his work and described him as *"...the rediscoverer of the totality and polarity of the human psyche and its striving for unity: the diagnostician of the crisis of man in the age of science and technology; the interpreter of the primeval symbolism and of the individuation of mankind.* [81] Jung's prophetic contribution to our culture and our times is reflected in this statement.

TOLKIEN'S COMPENSATORY MYTH FOR OUR TIMES

Jung believed that culture transforms through the individuation of individuals and their creative lives as well as the creative production of genuine artists. Tolkien was an exceptional example of how creative output can have a healing effect on culture and be a light-beam for deeper cultural transformation. He perfectly fits Jung's description of "the artist," especially the visionary type, "[who] is not a person endowed with free will who seeks his own ends, but one who allows art to realize its purposes through him.[82] As a human being he may have moods and a will and personal aims, wrote Jung, but as an artist he is "man" in a higher sense - he is "collective man," a vehicle and moulder of the unconscious psychic life of mankind."

Tolkien was such a "collective man" who was aware of what it means to be an instrument for a higher Will and, by way of his art, he

---

[81] As reported in Merrill Berger and Stephen Segaller, 2000, p. 10

[82] 1966, p. 101

is having a large, albeit still unconscious effect on the psychic life of Western humankind. Although millions of people throughout the world enjoy Tolkien's legendarium, few understand the potentially formative influence of his work on the consciousness of our times. Indeed, his works, at least as of 1998, are rarely taught, even in the conventional sense as literature.[83] There is no evidence that I know of that suggests there has been any appreciable change since then.

Tolkien believed that, through what he referred to as sub-creation, one can create a secondary world that is a reflection, or a glimpse of the truth inherent in the created Primary World of daily life.[84] Although it would be a world of fantasy, authentic sub-creation still, however, needs to reflect the phenomenon of our conscious life. In order to command belief, according to Tolkien, the making of such a Secondary World of Fantasy, not only requires "strangeness and wonder arising from the freedom from the observed fact," but reference to the Primary World we live in, as well as "the inner consistency of reality.[85]" This secondary world, in Tolkien's opinion, must therefore be "credible, commanding Secondary Belief," while combining the ordinary, the extraordinary, the fictitious and the actual.[86]

All the requirements Tolkien listed for developing a Secondary World of Fantasy are fulfilled in an exemplary fashion in *The Lord of the Rings*. When immersed in the epic drama, for all extents and purposes, one is immersed in a real world with real events that demand emotional involvement. It is a real world of extraordinary events, of beauty and terror, of tragedy and comedy, of chivalry and heroism, of magic and drudgery, of the joyful turn of events, what Tolkien called eucatastrophe, and catastrophe, of fellowship and mutual trust and betrayal, of grief, suffering and pain, of pathos and Eros, of creative Good and destructive Evil.

Hobbits and the Shire could refer to country life in rural England

---

[83] Joseph Pearce, 1998

[84] Joseph Pearce, 1998

[85] As reported in Paul H. Kocker, 1972, p. 1

[86] Ibid

and the dark, scientific and technological worlds of Sauron and Saruman find reflection in industrialized northern England. There is, in addition, extraordinary erudition and attention to detail in Tolkien's development of different languages for different races, Men and Hobbits, Elves, Dwarves and Ents, as well as the Black Speech of Sauron and Orcs, with each language reflecting the culture and values of the speakers. It is noteworthy that these languages were not invented but discovered, which helps explain their artistic and psychological authenticity. In fact, Tolkien's use of languages and choice of names is always significant and made with well-considered feeling-evaluation, for which reason I indicate the meaning of each name and source language when it is first encountered in the essay.

There are two Elf languages, Quenya (Elf-Quenya: 'speech'), which is closest to the original Elf language and more lyrical, and Sindarin (Elf-Quenya: 'grey-elven'), which is still beautiful. There is also a common tongue, a phenomenon reflective of the contemporary world, where English or, less often French, serves in this capacity. There is a real sense of history with dates and the reckoning of historical time back to the First Age of Man and the Elder days; and the felt-need to be connected to one's ancestors and their traditions for the sake of both individual integrity and cultural wholeness. This is a particularly relevant message to the contemporary post-modern world, where we believe we can and ought to revise society and cultural norms every generation.

In fact, there have been several notable discontinuities in Western culture throughout its glorious and troubled history, right up until the present day. There is, for instance, a danger of completely jettisoning the truths of our Christian heritage for the sake of a narrowly defined "liberal" reason, what, Henri de Lubac refers to as "atheistic humanism.[87]" Atheistic humanism is based on intellectual, moral and cultural relativism without the guiding presence of a supreme Deity. During the time Christianity became integrated in Western culture there was repression of the pagan worldview, which may well have been necessary for the sake of the development of moral consciousness and Christian humanism. It is now, however, essential

---

[87] As reported in George Weigel, 2005

to re-assimilate the pagan sensibility to consciousness without losing the cultural advance made thanks to the Christian spirit. In contemporary terms, this means that there is a need to re-connect to the archetypal and instinctual substratum of the psyche, in the case of a few individuals, personally and consciously by way of the individuation process. Otherwise, it ideally needs to be done through the culture, something which is, at the moment, discouraged because of our society's extreme one-sidedness.

As a cultural antidote, it is noteworthy that Tolkien has managed to fully accommodate and uplift paganism in his mythological drama, as well as account for the evolution of consciousness in his four Ages of Man, while retaining the highest Christian values and virtues. The significance of this achievement and its potential value may be better appreciated when one understands that Nazi Germany is an example of a nation that was overwhelmed by the pagan psyche and, as a consequence, suffered a cultural psychosis with well-known devastating results.[88] In fact, it is particularly interesting to note that the compensatory pagan mythology informing Tolkien's *The Lord of the Rings* is in large part Nordic, which is, of course, Germany's underlying pre-Christian mythological psyche as well.

In England, *The Lord of the Rings* has been acclaimed "'the greatest book of the century'" and Britain's "favorite book of any century," giving evidence to the fact that it touches people at a deep psychological level.[89] Its poignancy is due to the fact that the story combines distant times and archetypal reality of mythical dimensions with the ordinary, down to earth life of the common person to which we can all relate. As will become more evident as I go along, I am not using the words "myth" and "mythical" in the sense they are normally understood today, as an untruth or illusion, but as story involving supernatural forces and beings. The enduring popularity of *The Lord of the Rings* is testimony to the authenticity of Tolkien's work and confirmation that he was not "inventing" a story or myth but, as he declared, he always had the sense of "'recording what was actually "there."[90]

---

[88] C. G. Jung, 1970b
[89] Joseph Pearce, 1998, pp. 1, 3
[90] As reported in Timothy O'Neil, 1979, p. 157

Tolkien believed that true fantasy most effectively propagated recovery or clear seeing and truth because of the immediacy of images and forms rather than argument through concepts and abstract ideas. This view parallels Jung's[91] position regarding thinking in primordial images and his pithy observation that "concepts are coined and negotiable values; images are life." Clear seeing, Tolkien proposed, leads to "freedom from possessiveness," a phenomenon that involves withdrawal of projections and living more in harmony with the archetypal ground of being.[92] Conscious relatedness to the primordial symbolic worlds, which make up the foundation of the psyche, does carry one beyond normal complex-ridden connections to people, animals and objects, and allows one to experience and relate to life in a more objective fashion. Indeed, according to Jung, "It is only possible to live the fullest life when we are in harmony with these symbols; wisdom is a return to them."[93]

In agreement with Joseph Campbell's observation on the derivation of myth, Tolkien's work developed from his inner vision and what he referred to as an exploration of the primal world of Faërie.[94] In fact, Tolkien originally set out to write a myth for England, which he believed it did not have. In his opinion, its importance lay in the fact that "legends and myths are largely made of 'truth'" that point to transcendent facts in a way that is otherwise impossible.[95] According to Campbell, not only are myths vehicles for transpersonal forces, they also serve various important functions that, I suggest, can also be attributed to Tolkien's legendarium.[96] The first is that, inasmuch as *The Lord of the Rings* and *The Silmarillion* implicitly refer to life in the contemporary world, including an unsentimental description of the forces of good and evil, it reconciles consciousness to the nature of life.

Campbell's second function is realized in Tolkien's work by the

---

[91] 1974a, p.180

[92] 1979, p. 59

[93] As reported in Jacobi and Hull, editors, p. 47

[94] 2004a

[95] As reported in Joseph Pearce, 1998, p. 61

[96] 2005b, 2005c

explanatory nature and awe one feels in the nature of his description of a cosmos with both good and evil forces; a cosmos ultimately designed by Illúvatar (Quenya: 'all-father'), the Transcendent One. His cosmos is not only highly ordered, but created by the Valar, the thoughts of the One, gods or angels of other traditions, and marred by the rebellion of the mightiest and most knowledgeable Valar, originally known as Melkor and later as Morgoth (Elf-Sindarin: dark enemy).[97] This is a similar explanation for the origin of a counter-Will as the one given by Christianity in the purported rebellion of the Jewish and Christian God's most beautiful angel and right hand man, Lucifer.

In Tolkien's mythology, the Valar consist of the fourteen Ainur (Elf-Quenya: holy ones), the powers of the One, who become involved in Eä (Elf-Quenya: Imperative of to be), the Creation, of which there are seven females and seven males.[98] His complex cosmos also includes the incarnation of lesser Ainur known as Maiar, whose task was to tend Arda or the Earth, which was intended to be the home of the children of Illúvatar. There were also Istari, of whom Gandalf counts as an important incarnation, Tolkien referred to as Valar "of a sort," possibly Maiar, who incarnated on Middle-earth to guide the Free People [Wizards, Elves, Men, Dwarves, Ents and Hobbits] in their dealings with Sauron.[99] Two of them, Sauron and the Balrog rebelled during the First Age to serve Melkor disobeying this injunction. They were joined in the Third Age by the chief Istari, Saruman, whose self-serving purpose was ultimately in service of disharmony and destruction and the dark force of Morgoth.

Although the Valar were involved in putting order in the cosmos and were directly involved in the affairs of Middle-earth they were instructed not to control the destinies of the Free People, but to allow them the exercise of free will. This was particularly evident with the children of Illúvatar, Elves, the Firstborn, and Men, the Second born and Younger Children, [and Hobbits] explaining their sense of independence, free-will

---

[97] Robert Foster, 1978, passim

[98] 1999b.

[99] Robert Foster, 1978, p. 281.

and concern about destiny. A significant goal for the coming Fourth Age is the marriage of Elves to humans, creating off-springs with the qualities of both races.

Finally, the characteristics of the Dwarves and their unique qualities and challenges are understandable given Tokien's description of their creator Father, the Smith-Valar, Aulë.[100] He created the Dwarves in secret outside of the knowledge of either his spouse, Yavanna (Elf-Quenya; fruit giver, giver of fruits) or Illúvatar, the One. He fabricated them prior to the latter's creation of Elves and Men, out of impatience in waiting for the fulfillment of the One's design, and desire for Children to teach his crafts and knowledge. He made them unyielding and strong, with great power of endurance in order to counteract the pervasive presence of Melkor.

The Dwarves ancestry goes back to Seven Fathers, and a feminine origin seems to have been excluded from the essence of their being. Yet Aulë later reconciled with both Illúvatar, who granted the Dwarves the right to existence, and his spouse, Yavanna, also known as Kementári, Queen of the Earth, the primary care-giver and guardian of all things that grow especially the olvar.[101] Moreover the Dwarves' home and work halls in valleys, caves and inside mountains imply containment in the Earth Mother. Their love of beauty and attachment to gold suggests the psychological importance of assimilating their earth-related values to consciousness.

In fact, Aulë had submitted his creation to the Will of Illúvatar. Thus, when life is lived in harmonious relationship with archetypal and instinctual reality, Dwarves are secret and creative workers for the Great Mother and a boon to life in Middle-earth. In this regard, it is noteworthy that both Melkor and Aulë were similar in their knowledge of substance and mastery of craft although the former was impatient, jealous and hungry for power, while Aulë was both humble and compassionate. Their similar talents is no doubt related to the fact that, with the rise of the dark force, the Balrog and Orcs took possession of

---

[100] 1999b.

[101] Robert Foster, 1978

the Dwarves' home and work hall in Khaza-dûm, which later became known as the Mines of Moria (Elf-Sindarin: 'black pit'). They are perverted forces driven relentlessly to work for evil purposes and the destruction of life.

The third function of mythology is to provide a moral and sociological order, which in the case of Tolkien's mythology is clearly Christian, enhanced by Nordic valor and strength, Celtic sensitivity and Finnish naturalness in the context of contemporary England. In addition, a second birth beyond normal collective consciousness is described in the heroic journeys and individuation according to different soul-types personified by Gandalf, Aragorn, Frodo and Sam. I will discuss this in some detail below.

In full agreement with Tolkien's experience, according to Jung, we don't invent myth but it speaks to us "a word of God," and is "the revelation of a divine life in man."[102] Although Jung was speaking here about myth in general terms as a sacred and salutary phenomenon for the collective person and community, he was also referring to the need for individuals to develop a personal relationship to the mythological or archetypal ground of being. Their metaphysical task, he believed, involves raising consciousness by way of experiencing the clash of opposites in the psyche, which can be only accomplished by "mythologizing."[103]

The underlying archetypal pattern of *The Silmarillion,* which contains the background story for *The Lord of the Rings,* is the Fall of Man and Elves and all the Free People. Included are a wonderful creation myth, cosmology and accounting of the gods and goddesses, the origin of evil, the birth of the Dwarves, and the coming of the Elves and humans into Middle-earth, the dawn of light, the sun and moon Trees and their destruction by a giant spider, Ungoliant (Elf-Sindarin: dark spider), and Melkor. There is the subsequent creation of three splendid silmaril jewels that contain the original light from the Trees, covetousness and subsequent tragedies.

The fundamental design of *The Lord of the Rings* is based on the archetype of the life of Christ, a pattern that, in one way or another, is

---

[102] 1965, p. 340
[103] Ibid, p. 311

well reflected in the story of each of the four main heroes, Frodo, Sam, Aragorn and Gandalf. Tolkien himself noted that *The Lord of the Rings* is a Christian story, fundamentally "a religious and Catholic work," even though it took place during a pagan mythological age, well before the incarnation of Christ and the Christian epoch.[104] Indeed, although the archetype of the life of Christ is fundamental and pervasive, there are other mythological themes that have been masterfully interwoven into the story, for instance, paradise, the myth of the hero, the heroic quest, descent to the underworld, return of the hero, the wise old man and woman, ritual inauguration of the king and queen and their eventual deaths, the planting of Trees of Light and the establishment of a renewed united kingdoms and rejuvenated (Hobbit) community and finally, the main theme of *The Lord of the Rings*, realization of immortality and journey to the Undying lands. Although none of the hero figures was meant to be an allegorical representation of Christ *per se*, they each represent different soul types that go through a process of individuation and "Christification," each according to his own propensities and capacity. Tolkien's differentiation of what can be referred to as the archetype of the life of Christ is remarkable, giving image and form to Jung's observation that "what happens in the life of Christ happens always and everywhere."[105] Everybody can relate to that to some degree in their personal lives, some people more consciously than others, although most often through the experience of life's suffering, sorrow and vital joy, and not so much through the transformation of conscious individuation.

Tolkien regarded Christianity as the "True Myth," inasmuch as the basic archetypal pattern of a dying and resurrecting god was fully embodied on earth in the life of Christ.[106] Yet he loved pagan mythologies and especially incorporated Nordic, Celtic and Finnish mythological themes in his legendarium, believing that these "lesser myths" still referred to experiential truths of the human condition and "derive from Reality or

---

[104] 1981, p. 172

[105] 1975a, p. 89

[106] As reported in Joseph Pearce, 1998, p. 105

are flowing into it."[107] He, in fact, believed these particular mythologies reflect the psyche of people in North-Western Europe.

Tolkien's creative life was recognizably influenced by a recurrent dream of a Great Wave that rolled over "the trees and green fields," and from which he woke gasping for breath.[108] He recounted that the dream came "beginning with memory," and he referred to it as his "Atlantis-haunting" dream, implying relatedness to the distant ancestral past of Atlantis and pagan mythology.[109] He discovered that it was through his creative writing that the dream gradually subsided. As Verlyn Flieger astutely observes, in the guise of Gondor and its reference to Númenor, the city which was drowned for reasons of its grandiose spiritual ambitions, like the legendary Atlantis, "the ghost of Atlantis and the Great Wave haunts *The Lord of the Rings.*"[110] The epic struggle that takes place at the end of the Third Age is to re-establish the glory of Gondor (Elf-Sindarin: 'stone-land') and for Aragorn to assume his rightful place as King.

The redemption of paganism is revealed by the fact that, in terms of virtues, *The Lord of the Rings* is imbued with Christian values, such as the four cardinal virtues of the Middle Ages, prudence, justice, fortitude and temperance as well as honor, obedience and faithfulness.[111] Moreover, an important ingredient in everybody's individual development in the story is moral choice, free will and self-sacrifice, and this in the context of an ordered universe. Needless to say, as well as beneficent choice based on integrity of purpose, free-will can lead to inferior moral choice, perhaps even for evil. In fact, there are many examples of both types of choice in *The Lord of the Rings,* as well as the consequences.

By and large, in the pre-Christian and pre-classical pagan world, the gods/goddesses ruled; the supreme ruler in ancient Greece being Zeus, and the then current belief was that the best course in life was to bow to one's

---

[107] Ibid
[108] As reported in Verlyn Flieger, 1997, p. 4
[109] Ibid, p. 76
[110] Ibid, p. 196
[111] Ralph C. Wood, 2003

fate, which was ultimately Zeus' Will. There was cosmic order but no free will, the belief being that the stars ruled destiny and one was obliged to submit to the procession of the gifts and poisons of *heimarmene* or fate.[112] One of the eventual outcomes of the rejection of the pagan worldview was repression of the gods/goddesses, which coincide with the repression of archetypal and instinctive aspects of a full life. The gods and goddesses became diseases, and, in the contemporary world, they also manipulate us in increasingly sophisticated way through propaganda, advertising, public relations and other means of dominating the play of life. Although we believe in free will and moral choice, we have, as a culture, little sense of cosmic order, and virtually no conscious recognition of its existence and the implications. Nonetheless, I believe that more people have some experience of it through synchronicity than is generally acknowledged.

Synchronicities or meaningful coincidences, where inner and outer worlds are in evident harmony, are conscious personal experiences of cosmic order or general acausal orderdness, which involves new creations in time and the initiative of a higher will. *The Lord of the Rings* is full of such synchronicities, examples of personal experiences of cosmic order; yet the role of free will and moral choice is never abrogated. One particularly fine example takes place when, at the council of Elrond, where the fate of the Ring of Power was discussed by representatives of Free People, Frodo made a free choice to become the Ring-bearer, despite his declaration that he did not know the way.

There had been no pressure from Elrond (Elf-Sindarin: 'star dome'), a high Elf of penetrating power and wisdom who presided over the council, or anybody else to do so. Yet, once he accepted his burden, Elrond declared: "I think this path is appointed for you, Frodo...it is a heavy burden.....I do not lay it on you...But, if you take it freely, I will say that your choice is right."[113] Frodo was *called* in the sense of finding his vocation, in which case, there is free-will in harmony with what may be referred to as a higher cosmic order, a higher destiny. Later, when in the Elf refuge at Lothlórien and, after gazing into the mirror of Galadriel, which reveals past, present

---

[112] Hans Jonas, 1972

[113] Tolkien, 2005a, p. 353

and future possibilities, he understood that his life had become involved in a great history that includes shadow and sorrow as much as joy.[114]

Sam also eventually grew into this realization on the stairs of Cirith Ungol (Elf-Sindarin: 'pass of the spider'), where it dawned on him that they were part of the same tale as Man's distant ancestral hero and elf-friend, Beren. Typical of somebody with superior Eros and feeling, Sam's awareness of participating in a greater story involved a sense of being personally connected to other individuals, in this case, a human ancestor from the distant past. The latter lived during the First Age of Man, entered Angband (Elf-Sindarin: 'iron prison') with his beautiful and courageous elfin spouse, Lúthien (Elf-Sindarin), and managed to seize and escape with a Silmaril (Elf-Quenya: 'brilliance or jewel of silima; Elf-Quenya: 'shinning substance made by craft') from the Iron Crown of Sauron. The story, involving humanity's eternal struggle for Good and the conquest of Evil is as old as time.

Like Jung, Tolkien embraced a cultural reality that accepts our pagan nature, although not with blind adherence to fate, but rather with the potential to consciously uplift it through free-will and moral choice. His conscious values and beliefs were fully Christian; however, Christian without suppressing the high values and beliefs that are intrinsic to the pagan world view and natural order. Tolkien was always sympathetically concerned with humans *on earth* after the Fall of Man and therefore recognized the need to integrate the pagan cosmos of archetypal good and evil along with the notion of free will and moral choice.

Tolkien admitted that the work of artists affects their personal life, his included, but he was reticent to indicate how or how much his art was related to his own experience of personality transformation. He writes "An author cannot of course remain wholly unaffected by his experience, but the ways in which a story-germ uses the soil of experience, are extremely complex, and to define the process are at best guesses from evidence that is inadequate and ambiguous.[115] He considered it virtually impossible to determine the nature of the relationship between his art and his personal life.

---

[114] Verlyn Flieger, 1997
[115] Joseph Pearce,1998, p. 12

One thing, however, is beyond doubt; that Tolkien was *called* to write *The Lord of the* Rings and his other mythological writings and he took up the burden of his destiny. As Jung wrote, the genuine artist is not "endowed with free will who seeks his own ends, but one who allows art to realize its purpose through him…. – he is "collective man," a vehicle and moulder of the unconscious psychic life of mankind.[116] As I mentioned above, this was certainly the case of Tolkien; although not yet so evident, I believe it will become more so with time.

Until the 17th century, alchemy was an attempt to compensate for Christianity, which ruled on the surface and in people's conscious life, with pagan values, ultimately, to serve the redemption of spirit in matter. According to Jung, "it endeavours to fill in the gaps left open by the Christian tension of opposites."[117] In a like manner, Tolkien's opus compensates the contemporary post-modern relativistic world, ruled by science-technology and consumerism, with both Christian and uplifted pagan values and perceptions of the world. His prophetic voice is a definite moulder of psychic life today and, I would argue, the more consciously we take it up individually and as a society, the better. His prophetic message can clearly be an important ingredient in the individuation of Western culture and help provide it with an enlarged and enlightened container.

THE SELF AND THE DEEPER MEANING OF *THE LORD OF THE RINGS*

Tolkien insisted that there was a deeper meaning to his epic than the question of giving up power and dominion over others or war or otherwise. The real theme for him concerned Death and Immortality and the mystery of human love for the world. Yet, in his mythology, Men are doomed to die, while the Elves have effective immortality in life, more

[116] 1966, p. 101
[117] As reported in Marie-Louise von Franz, 1975, p. 216

precisely enduring life, yet anguish over the doom of not being able to leave Middle-earth until evil is vanquished and the story complete.[118]

Elves are contained in a world of eternal time, although not true immortality, which involves a relationship to the infinite, the Self beyond time. Elves and their surroundings are an aspect of the generally unchanging archetypal world, embodying fundamental structural blueprints for apprehending life and dynamically living it. In their purity of being they are contained in the relatively timeless space of paradise, still somewhat represented by the High Elves of Lothlórien (Elf-Sindarin: blossom-dream-land'). It is noteworthy that, there, they still held the Valar in high regard, and had special reverence for Varda (Elf-Quenya: 'the exalted'), the mightiest feminine power of the One, usually known in Middle-earth as Elbereth (Elf-Sindarin: 'star- queen'). Moreover, their food, *lembas* (Elf-Sindarin: 'way-bread'), indicative of the kind of psychological and spiritual nourishment they imparted, was not only tasty and remained fresh for many days but transformative in that it enhanced life and the positive feeling for life. It was, in other words, sustenance for the soul, soul-food and could be referred to as Eucharistic, in both its unifying aspect and its involvement in redemption.

The natural inclinations and gifts of these Elves indicate the primacy of their vertical connection and relationship with cosmic powers. The other principal group of Elves in *The Lord of the Rings* lived in Rivendell, where they kept a more integral connection with the other free people and events in Middle-earth. Their interests lay in a more horizontal direction although, there continued to be a memory of the more timeless archetypal connection.

These two groups of Elves incarnate two fundamental expressions of the evolutionary aspect of the human soul, which Sri Aurobindo and the Mother referred to as the psychic being.[119] According to their teachings, the psychic being, or Self behind the heart, is the incarnated portion of the eternal individual soul or Self, which experiences life from incarnation to

---

[118] Verlyn Flieger, 1997
[119] 1997

incarnation. Because of its direct interrelatedness with the Self, it retains a natural vertical link to its non-incarnated parent. It is the differentiated aspect of the individual Self that is involved in the natural world and relates directly to the archetypal psyche. The psychic being is an expression of the central flame that ignites human individuation and the transformation of human nature. It naturally inclines towards truth of being and purity of intention, and knows through feeling.

Elves from both Rivendell and Lothlórien, especially the latter, live relatively close to the psychic being and strove to incarnate its values and propensities, although they could be tempted by Evil. In fact, since their exile from the Uttermost West and the Undying Lands, there have not only been battles and heroic action taken against Morgoth, but there have also been examples of strife between Elves and Elves, mainly stimulated by the lust for power and the possession of the Silmarils, the three resplendent jewels containing the original light of the Two Trees, the light of creation and the Imperishable Fire, fashioned by the Elf, Fëanor (Elf-Sindarin/Quenya: 'Spirit of Fire). Inasmuch as the microcosm and the macrocosm are fundamentally identical the attitude, values and skills of the Elves, in fact, represent qualities that are potentially integral to human life. Personally and consciously relating to the archetype deepens one's experience of life and culture and is an essential ingredient in healing and the individuation process as defined by Jung.

Basic principles and patterns of life generally do not change, hence their relative timelessness. When world culture experiences major aeonic shifts, like in our present day, however, they coincidentally do go through a metamorphosis, initiated by an acausal factor that embraces and transcends the manifest world. This is reflected in a fundamental transformation of consciousness, which Jung beautifully articulated as: "we are living in what the Greeks called the *kairos* – the right moment- for a 'metamorphosis of the gods,' of the fundamental principles and symbols."[120] This refers to the fact that "the unconscious man within us is changing," a phenomenon that in itself transcends human consciousness and will.

---

[120] 1970a, p. 304

In psychological terms, individuation not only requires a personal relationship to the archetypal psyche but also a relationship with the central archetype, the Self. The Self or wholeness is paradoxically both the center of the psyche and the archetypal psyche itself and can be symbolized by the number Four [4]. It is not only instrumental in initiating the individuation process itself, but, by way of the individual Self and its delegate, the psychic being, it is the integrative factor *par excellence* that cajoles the psyche towards more differentiated wholeness and eventually a life more directly in its service. Immortality has nothing to do with seemingly endless time, but involves the sacrifice of the ego to the psychic being and relationship with the infinite Self.

The challenge confronting Tolkien was the relationship between the archetypal worlds of the Elves and the normal space and time-bound world of Men on Middle-earth. His mythology foresaw the need for "the Elven strain to enter Men for the ennoblement of the Human Race, from the beginning destined to replace the Elves."[121] Tolkien understood that the eventual answer was intermarriage between destined members of the two races, Men and Elves, which, symbolically, amounts to humans gaining the capacity to access the Self behind the heart, the psychic being, and the archetypal psyche, while remaining fully responsible to the conditions of Middle-earth. This leads to a personal and conscious relationship between both the psychic being and the archetypal psyche, with the eventuality of connecting to the cosmic and transcendent Self, portrayed by the fact that the High Elves continued to honor the primary feminine power of the One, Varda, whom they usually propitiated as Elbereth.

The challenge of the Fourth Age of Man is conscious individuation and bridging the inner archetypal worlds into space and time. This, according to Tolkien, requires giving up power and dominion while opening up to feminine Eros, which relates one to the fullness of life. Jung held a similar view and noted how Jesus collided with the "power-intoxicated devil of the prevailing Caesarian psychology" and "fulfilled his Messianic mission by pointing out to humanity the old truth that where

---

121 Verlyn Flieger, 1983, p. 145

force [power] rules there is no love and where love reigns force does not count."[122] Individuation and finding one's unique place in life also requires forging a relationship to the infinite, while being meaningfully involved in life.

The ubiquitous Four (4) that pervades *The Lord of the Rings* and the high value Tolkien gave to Eros and feeling throughout is consistent with his contention that the deeper message of the epic concerns relationship with the Self and Immortality. Making such a connection requires death of ego and its power-driven goals like in the *Katha Upanishad*, where *Yama*, the Lord of Death is teacher and guide, ultimately for the sake of consciousness and the incarnation of the Self in life.[123] Understood as the chief organizer of the phenomenal world, he is well-positioned to reveal the mystery of karmic interrelationships, both individual and collective, as well as death and immortality. Tolkien understood what J. M. Barrie, the author of *Peter Pan*, failed to realize. The latter left Peter Pan in *Never-Never Land* where he lives a timeless life, not wanting to return to the normal everyday world and grow up. Psychologically, this pattern is rather ubiquitous today, especially amongst some men, or a hidden aspect of men, who fail to mature psychologically and live an uncommitted, transitional and irresponsible life.

The Ring of Power: A Symbol of the Self

Three Rings for the Elven-kings under the sky,
Seven for the Dwarf-lords in their halls of stone,
Nine for Mortal Men doomed to die,
One for the Dark Lord on his dark throne
In the land of Mordor where the Shadows lie.
One ring to rule them all, One Ring to find them,
One ring to bring them all and in the darkness bind them
In the land of Mordor where the Shadows lie.

---

[122] 1974b, pp. 180, 181
[123] V. Madhusudan Reddy, 1985

The Ring of Power is directly connected to the evil will of Sauron and brings the bearer of the Ring into relationship to him. Yet, it is not simply a symbol of Evil, but more deeply a symbol of the Self and wholeness, indicated by the fact that it is formed out of gold, the incorruptible metal, itself a symbol of the Self and the fact that it is beautiful, circular, perfectly balanced and has an affinity with fire. Fire illuminates the Black Speech of Mordor, which is engraved on the Ring, so that it become a fiery inscription, found both inside and out, making the Ring manifest as union of opposites and perfect symbol of the Self. All fire is born from the Imperishable Flame of creation and, like gold, is a symbol of the Self. In fact, although the Dark Lord, Sauron, was the master architect, he tricked the Elvin Noldorin (Elf-Quenya: from Noldor: knowledgeable) smiths of Eregion (Elf-Sindarin: 'holly-region') to contribute their skills, knowledge and goodness into helping him forge the Ring.

Although Sauron was the chief fabricator of the Ring, he himself did not fully comprehend how it functioned, as it was ultimately subject to a higher Will, the Will of Illúvatar, the One. All Rings, those of the Elves, Dwarves and Men, which were forged by the Noldorin Elves, were ultimately dependent on the Master Ring, the key being that the "*One Ring*" had the power "*to bring them all and in the darkness bind them/ In the land of Mordor where the Shadows lie.*"[124] Connected to the earth, even a perverse earth, the One Ring of power had the capacity of coagulation or binding.

Bearing the Ring draws one inexorably and increasingly into relationship with the Shadow and Evil. Yet, Frodo's quest involved the unmaking of the Ring through surrendering power ambition by tossing it into the Fire of Doom, which burned in the depths of the Crack of Doom, for its dissolution. The quest also drew forces of good and Free People together in search of freedom, truth and justice, and fellowship. The One Ring's power of binding is related to the earth and the alchemical *coagulatio*, which, psychologically, refers to the capacity to consciously realize inner experiences in life. This power resided with the Dark Lord

---

[124] Timothy O'Neil, 1979, p. 131

and his minions, whose home is in '*Mordor where the Shadows lie.*' There was a need to consciously assimilate one's relationship to Shadow values in order to realize the Self in life and bring in the Fourth Age of Man. Related to this is the need for Man to internalize his relationship to Elves and their sensibilities, as they, along with Gandalf, will leave for the Undying lands once the Ring of Power has been surrendered.

The Ring is the central focus of *The Lord of the Rings* and, when it is worn, it draws the wearer into the world of Sauron and Evil, as one disappears from view in the normal world. Symbolically, this suggests that the wearer becomes invisible to others because of their lack of comprehension of the nature of archetypal Evil that is being experienced. As I argue above, the Ring of Power, however, is not a symbol of Evil alone, but it is also related to wholeness and the power of creative manifestation.

Tolkien's epic in this regard is fully compatible with Jung's discoveries on the nature of the individuation process. Along with consciously connecting to spiritual energy *per se* through the Self as well as with positive archetypal forces of life and renewal, Jung recognized a need to increasingly integrate considerable personal shadow as well as relationship to the archetypal or collective Shadow. Wholeness demands that this should be the case. Without personal shadow and a conscious relationship to the collective Shadow, psychological and spiritual realization remains ethereal and unrelated to the manifest world and culture.

The Shadow is simply the unconscious psyche, and, from a psychological perspective, there are two aspects that one needs to come to terms with, each in a different way. One aspect is related to personal and/or collective repression that is ideally brought to consciousness and assimilated to life, which has become terribly one-sided and dissociated. The repression of the positive aspects of paganism fit this category, and they need to be once again joyously accepted in our personal and collective lives for the sake of reinvigoration. Tolkien's world includes such beliefs, attitudes and values in his description of Elves, Ents (Old English: 'giant'), Tom Bombadil, Goldberry, Gandalf and synchronicity and the play of nature.

Understanding the nature of Ents, the tree-herds, is of particular interest. They are depicted as self-reflective beings that evolved from trees that looked like a fourteen-foot cross between a tree and a man, which could move horizontally. They were originally wakened by the Elves, who both taught them to speak and communicated empathetically with them, indicating a sympathetic relationship between Ents and Elves. They represent healthy instincts of the psychosomatic psyche and the autonomic nervous system, the vital-physical that have become somewhat humanized thanks to the influence of the incarnated soul and psychic being.

Tragically, sometime in the First or Second Age, the male Ents and Entwives became estranged as the Entwives preferred plants, small trees, flowering trees and gardens, and taught agriculture to Men, while the Male Ents preferred larger trees and roaming throughout their territory that stretched from the Old Forest to Fangorn (Elf-Sindarin: 'beard-tree') Forest. It was named after the oldest living Ent, Fangorn, also known as Treebeard during the time of the War of the Rings. This indicates a fundamental disharmony between the male and female psyches at the level of the autonomic nervous system, something that most students of life would readily agree upon. Men are typically more naturally related to the assertive propensities of the sympathetic nervous system, while women are generally more naturally connected to the more passive parasympathetic system. Healing for either sex as well as the relationship between men and women involves consciously coming to terms with and being rooted in both the sympathetic and parasympathetic nervous systems. That would be symbolically related to reconciliation between the Ents and the Ent wives.

The attributes and qualities assigned to the creative hard working introverted earth-bound Dwarf, who carries the projection of "the ugliest man" shadow for the European and North American psyche, and rejected accordingly, in particular, needs to be integrated. This pejorative projection on Dwarves and their qualities of being is clearly depicted in Nietzsche's *Thus Spake Zarathustra*, when the spiritual Zarathustra, in his hubris, talked down to the Dwarf, who has spoken words from a deep well of wisdom in response to the formers haughty talk about two different paths of life, one going forward, the other backwards: "'Everything straight lieth," murmured the Dwarf contemptuously. All truth is crooked; time itself is a circle." Zarathustra replied to the Dwarf, saying: "'Thou spirit of gravity!" said I wrathfully, "do not take it too lightly! Or I shall let thee squat where thou squattest, Haltfoot,- and I carried thee high!'"[125]

Here the spiritual man believed he carried the Dwarf to spiritual heights but, as Jung observed, the reverse is true; "the dwarf is really... .Zarathustra's higher mind."[126] The Dwarf represents the inferior function, the full confirmation of which leads to the portals of knowledge and wisdom, a truth often depicted in Fairy Tales in that it is the clumsy and ill-adapted brother who marries the princess or finds the treasure. Recognition of the need for this acceptance is essential for the contemporary culture of privilege that has severed its connection to its ancestral roots and spiritual earth. True ideals and values of creative renewal can only be integrated and brought into manifest reality through hard work, perseverance and endurance,- the spirit of gravity, attributes typically assigned to the mythological Dwarf.

The other aspect of the Shadow needs to be rejected; and this is the side related to the ambitious drive for power, dominion and possessiveness, so wonderfully described by Tolkien in his depiction of Sauron, Sauruman, the Balrog, the Orcs and Uruk-Hai, and Gollum. In *The Lord of the Rings*, it is, however, never simply a question of the battle of Good vs. Evil *per se*, but of the effect of evil on life, on nature and the Free People of Middle-earth, including the Istari, like Saruman and the Balrog. Men like Wormtongue and Théoden, Dwarves, who have lost their home, Hobbits, especially Gollum, and Elves, some of whom have been changed into Orcs by Sauron and Saruman and finally the Ents who have become Huorns after the Great Darkness. Tolkien's descriptive image of these beings and their perversions is an archetypal rendition of what happens to life in the world when dark forces of dissociation, disunity and the power drive dominate. Seen, from the point of view of the unconscious, I, in fact,

---

[125] Nietszche, as reported in C. G. Jung, 1988, p. 1271
[126] 1988, p. 1271

believe that this is a pretty reliable picture of our one-sided dissociated way of thinking and acting, and its effect upon life and nature.

The distinction between shadow spiritual figures and leadership figures, such as Saruman, Wormtongue and Théoden, and perverted dynamic shadow forces such as the Balrog, Uruk-hai and Orcs can be profitably made. The former relate to perverted values, attitudes, belief systems and codes of conduct, the latter to perverted instinctual drives. The Huorns represent disordered aspects of the autonomic nervous system, a phenomenon connected to our highly civilized and repressed world, which is out of touch with nature. Gollum represents the Hobbits' shadow inasmuch as he represents a soul which has been occluded by perverted values, attitudes, beliefs and drives, although in his alter-ego as Sméagol, the original decent hobbit occasionally made his appearance.

The challenge to individual integrity and the temptation of evil and disorder, moral choice and the consequences of one's choice occur over and over again in *The Lord of the Rings*. Except Tom Bombadil, the Original Man, and his spouse Goldberry, there is temptation for evil or disorder on every one of the Free Peoples including the Ents. Even Gandalf, the wizard and the high Elf-Queen, Galadriel, felt the terrible temptation of power, although they are able to reject it. Their responses to the temptation and the response of others, such as Baromir and Saruman, to the same temptation are particularly noteworthy.

When Frodo offered the Ring of Power to Gandalf as "wise and powerful," he exclaimed: "No!"....With that power I should have power too great and terrible. And over me the Ring would gain a power still greater and more deadly....Do not tempt me, for I do not want to become like the Dark Lord himself. Yet the way of the Ring to my heart is by pity, pity for weakness and the desire of strength to do good Tolkien."[127] Gandalf showed a high degree of objective awareness of his subjective propensity towards evil, his inferiority and portal to the temptation of power being pity for the plight of others and the desire to do good. He was therefore able to reject it. Later, Saruman cunningly appealed to Gandalf's spiritual

---

[127] 2005a, pp. 81, 82

vanity and high ideals by encouraging him to join him in siding with the growing Dark Power, saying: "And the Wise, such as you and I, may with patience come at last to direct its course, to control it. ….we can, argued Saruman, keep our thoughts in our hearts, deploring maybe evils done by the way, but approving the high and ultimate purpose: Knowledge, Rule, Order; all the things we have striven in vain to accomplish. ….There need not be, would not be any real change in our designs, only in our means."[128] Gandalf was able to recognize this seductive voice for what it was as coming from an emissary of Mordor, and reject it, despite the danger to his life. He was conscious of the fact that Sauruman, the former head of the White Council and chief Istari, had gradually been diverted from his mandate to propagate free will and freedom amongst the people of Middle-earth. He was aware that he had given in to the temptation for power, which involved control and dominion over others, where the ends justify the means. By facing Saruman and responding to him directly rejecting his specious argument, Gandalf objectively saw what he would become were he to give in to the charming cajoling of Saruman, and he was, consequently, able to remain true to his higher self.

Galadriel, too, was tempted by the Ring of Power when it was offered to her by Frodo, with the words "You are wise and fearless and fair, Lady Galadriel….I will give you the One Ring, if you ask for it." She responded: "I do not deny that my heart has greatly desired to ask for what you offer….And now at last it comes. You will give me the Ring freely! In place of the Dark Lord you will set up a Queen. And I shall not be dark, but beautiful and terrible as the Morning and the Night! ….All shall love me and despair.[129]" Like Gandalf, Galadriel did not identify with her subjective nature, which is appealing to others, beautiful, strong and powerful, yet dreadful and terrible at the same time. She was able to see her propensities, her desire, her appeal and its effect on others, objectively. This allowed her to detach and make a moral choice for the Good.

It is interesting to compare Galadriel with Ayaesha, also known as *She*

---

[128] ibid, p. 338
[129] Ibid, pp. 475, 476

and *She-who-must-be-obeyed,* a principal personality in Rider Haggard's (1995) novel, *She.* Like Galadriel's self-description, Ayesha was described as beautiful and knowledgeable, as alluring yet terrible. Unlike Galadriel who, despite her love for Lothlórien, was destined and willing to leave Middle-earth on the unmaking of the Ring of Power, *She* was powerfully attached to enduring life. She also ruled by terror and dominion over others, so different from Galadriel, who rejected the use of power altogether and ruled through Eros. Unable to see her subjective nature objectively and obsessed with *Leo,* her lover in a past life, she blessed him with the very thing Galadriel rejected, the rule of power. Ayesha tried to seduce Leo with these fateful words: "Behold! Once more I kiss thee, and by this kiss, I give to thee dominion over sea and earth, over the peasant in his hovel, over the monarch in his palace halls, and cities crowned with towers, and those who breathe therein." Her designs were not fulfilled, however, and she shriveled up in the fire that she believed was meant to give her unending life. *Leo* and his companions were then able to escape and make their way back home. The difference between Ayesha and Galadriel is that the former identified with her natural feminine nature and passions, both good and evil, while Galadriel saw her nature in its entirety but, thanks to her connection to the soul and psychic being, she was able to detach from it, and make choices for the Good.

Attaining Power can be very tempting as Evil is often not indulged in for its own sake but for the sake of some alleged good. Not everybody has the integrity of Gandalf or Galadriel or has become so enveloped in the dark cloak of Power as Gollum or Saruman. Baromir, a courageous Captain of Gondor, is a case in point. He was proud and loved battle for its own sake and fought hard to protect his homeland of Minas Tirith and Gondor against the forces of Evil. He desired the Ring from the first moment that he was made aware of its existence and that Frodo's was the ring-bearer at the Council of Elrond. He justified his obsession with the rationale that he would use it against the Dark Lord in service of doing good and defeat the Enemy. After the Council of Elrond, Baromir finally confronted Frodo demanding to see the Ring, which he had glimpsed while in Rivendell. As Frodo was reluctant he argued beguilingly: "True-hearted Men, they will not be corrupted. We of Minas Tirith have been staunch through long years of trial. We do not desire the power of wizard-lords, only strength to defend ourselves, strength in a just cause. And behold! In our need chance brings to light the Ring of Power. It is a gift I say, a gift to the foes of Mordor. It is mad not to use it, to use the power of the enemy against him.[130]" Baromir's argument, agitated state and eventual demand that Frodo give him the Ring alarmed Frodo and incited him to put on the Ring of Power and disappear from view.

Baromir sought him frantically and with anger until he stumbled on a stone, fell to the ground and wept, realizing what he had done. He then called out to Frodo asking him to come back as "A madness took me, but it has passed."[131] The stone is a symbol of the Self, and his being caught by it and falling suggests that Baromir's soul understood that he had become possessed with desire for power and identified with his subjective nature, and therefore threw him down. He was not a whited-sepulcher and hypocrite but true to himself, although his identification with the personal shadow opened the door to his possession. In ancient Greece, heroes were often identified as suffering from *hamartia,* which has been translated as "tragic flaw" and James Hollis translated as "wounded vision."[132] Psychologically this refers to the inevitable limitation of one's worldview that are based on the intersecting dynamics that drive one's life such as genetics, family of origin and cultural influences, all which go into the formation of one's core complexes. These complexes are at the base of one's experience and view of life, which is inevitably one-sided, limited and flawed. This was the case of Baromir and he suffered accordingly.

Later on there was a search party to find Frodo, which included Baromir. He went off on his own and was eventually overcome by a party of evil Orcs. He fought bravely and killed several of them defending the hobbits, Merry and Pippin, but was eventually left for dead, pierced by many black Orc-arrows. Aragorn came upon him and Baromir confessed

---

[130] Ibid, p. 519
[131] Ibid, p. 521
[132] 2001, p. 14

his wrongdoing in his trying to take the Ring from Frodo, saying "I am sorry. I have paid."[133] He then bid Aragorn farewell, asking him to "go to Minas Tirith and save my people! I have failed."[134]

In this way Baromir not only acknowledged his moral failing that opened him to lust after the Ring, but he was fully accepting Aragorn as his leader and future King, something he had had difficulty doing. For these reasons Aragorn blessed him, declaring: "You have conquered. Few have gained such victory. Be at peace! Minas Tirith will not fail."[135] At that Baromir smiled, but did not speak again. Like Gandalf and Galadriel, he, too, was eventually able to see his subjective propensities objectively, including his pride and weakness in the face of the possibility of power, which opened the portal to possession and the attempt to seize the Ring of Power from Frodo. Part of Baromir's objective seeing relates to the fact that he was overpowered and killed by Orcs, which represent impulses of impatience and dissension that sow distrust and disunity, exactly what had overtaken him in his desire for the Ring and his threat to Frodo. Baromir's objective recognition of his character flaws and his sincere repentance brought Aragorn's blessing and healing, and his redemption.

The psychological task is assimilation of some shadow qualities and rejection of others and this requires moral discernment and choice, which is essential for individuation. According to Jung, the divine incarnation "only manifests in those relatively few individuals capable of enough consciousness to make ethical decisions, that is to decide for the Good."[136] Elsewhere Jung wrote that "the responsible living and fulfilling the divine will in us will be our form of worship and commerce with God. His Goodness means grace and light and His Dark side the terrible temptation of Power."[137] True moral choice has nothing to do with following a prescribed moral code, which in the final analysis is based

---

[133] p. 538

[134] Ibid

[135] Ibid

[136] As reported in Edward F. Edinger, 1996, p. 119

[137] Ibid

on professional and social convention and order. It is rather a question of personal conscience, which may in some cases appear identical to the moral code, but in all cases is based on a deeper inner reality that reconciles opposing viewpoints for a third position, which Jung referred to as the transcendent function.[138] It involves the influence of the soul and psychic being, which experiences the world feelingly and knows through feeling.

The transcendent function puts us in harmony with the divine will and Goodness, and, inasmuch as it involves reconciling opposing viewpoints, it also gives us an objective picture of our subjectivity allowing us to reject the temptation for power. Jung observed that "Man's sufferings did not derive from his sins but from the maker of his imperfections, the paradoxical God."[139] Edinger commented on this by saying, "the ego did not make itself [and] it is not responsible for its imperfections, its weaknesses, its lapse."[140] A good deal of our suffering is due to the fact that we identify with our subjectivity. But the ego is not responsible for the workings of the psyche and, as Jung wrote, "I must guard against identifying with my subjective experience.[141]" The ego's task then is to objectify its subjectivity through a process of dis-identification from it, in practice, through inner work, paying attention to one's dreams, doing active imagination and so on. Tolkien's depiction of the need for moral choice, the surrounding circumstances and arguments and the objectification of subjective responses in the case of Galadriel, Gandalf and Baromir, the dominant place he gave to feeling and the ultimate choice for good and rejection of power and dominion, are wonderful illustrations of this process. Included are both pagan *amor fati*, or love of one's fate, and also a moral choice for the Good.

---

[138] 1975b

[139] As reported in Edward Edinger, 1996 p. 115

[140] Ibid, p. 115

[141] ibid, p. 116

THE FOUR AGES OF MAN AND THE FOUR-FOLD PATH

From the point of view of individuation of the individual, Tolkien's *The Lord of the Rings* provides the reader with values, attitudes and beliefs as well as images of archetypal patterns and feelings that help understand the individuation process for the contemporary person. As I mentioned above, qualitatively understood, the number Four [4] is a symbol of wholeness and directly related to the Self and the goal of individuation, the transformation of personality and completeness of being. In the epic wholeness, to begin with, is indicated the fact that the hobbit's home community, the Shire, has four [4] divisions, north, south, east and west. This suggests that the hobbit's community and natural life is based on wholeness, although unconscious. The four-fold nature of the path of the quest, which is designed to develop consciousness, takes place in four geographical quadrants. The quest itself, in other words, requires circumscribing the Self for the sake of evolving individual conscious wholeness.

The underlying structure of wholeness is also indicated in the fact that, in Tolkien's legendarium, there are four ages reflecting the evolution of human consciousness.[142] The First Age can be described as the age of Elves and the realm of Faërie, where humans were relatively speaking unconscious and awkward. In the Second Age, there was considerable expansion of human consciousness along with the fall of the dark kingdom of Morgorth. Humans also illegitimately sought a deathless immortal life and their hubris resulted in the inundation of Númenor (from Elf-Quenya, Númenórë: 'west') and the drowning of many Númenoreans, the most noble and spiritually gifted of men during the Second Age. During the Third Age, consciousness and the unconscious were sundered, people lived in a one-sided way and there were many destructive influences affecting life. This reflects our experience of the world we currently inhabit. At the end of the War of the Rings fought between Sauron and the Free People, the Ring of Power was unmade and the Fourth Age, the Age

---

[142] Timothy R. O'Neil, 1979

of Man, promising harmony and integrity, was ushered in. As in Jung's understanding of the individuation process, wholeness as the goal of life is attained through conscious experience of the symbolic number Four [4], here symbolized as the Fourth Age of Man.

INDIVIDUATION: EARTH, AIR, FIRE AND WATER

At its most fundamental level, the process of individuation is reflected in the three rings of the Elves, one of water, one of air and one of fire, along with the One ruling Ring [of earth].[143] The High-Elf, Elrond wore the Ring of Air [Vilya (Quenya: 'air, sky')], which refers to healing touch and penetrating wisdom; the Elf-queen, Galadriel wore the Ring of Water [Nenya (Quenya: 'water-')], reflecting the womb of creation, especially with the light of Lórien; and Gandalf wore the Ring of Fire [Narya Quenya: 'fire-')], referring to sight and transformative renewal. The fourth Ring refers to the One [ruling] Ring, which was designed "to bring them all and in the darkness [of Mordor] bind them." Inasmuch as it was forged in the Crack of Doom, it is a Ring of Earth, bringing the number of Rings to four, the symbol of completeness.

This basic pattern of wholeness indicates that it is essential to include the earth for wholeness, which in *The Lord of the Rings*, is directly under the destructive influence of Evil and the Shadow. Alchemically, the earth is related to the state known as *coagulatio* and has the effect of binding and connecting one's realizations to ego consciousness and embodiment. Connecting one's psychological and spiritual realizations to the earth requires integration of the personal shadow and consciousness of one's relationship to the collective Shadow.

It is noteworthy that in *The Lord of the Rings* the Orcs and the fallen Maiar, the Balrog, a being with a black heart of dark fire and immense strength and intensity, have taken possession of the greatest of the ancient Dwarf Halls, the Mines of Moria, known in the language of the Dwarves,

---

[143] Robert Foster, 1978

as Khazad-dûm. The Orcs not only represent the impulse for dissension and moral degeneration they also hate anything beautiful. As the demon of might and terror, the Balrog represents the perverted engine of destruction in service to the Dark Lord. With the latter's reign and the influence of the Orcs, the creative impulses of the Dwarves and their natural talent for making beautiful objects, have been replaced by fear, the spirit of negation, long-smoldering anger, destruction and disunity along with ugliness.

The race which has the most positive and creative connection to the earth is the Dwarves, and three [3] of their Rings have been taken by the evil magician, Sauron, and four [4] have been lost or devoured by dragons. This is undoubtedly related to the isolated and cantankerous stubbornness of the Dwarves, their reciprocated distrust of other races, and their lust for possessions. Their redemption and transformation, however, is anticipated by the fact that the Dwarf Gimli is part of the fellowship working for the sake of good against evil and that he becomes fast friends with Legolas [Elf-Sindarin: 'green-leaf'], the Elf.

While in Lothlórien, Gimli realized loving feelings for the Elf-queen Galadriel and, when offered a gift from her, he uncharacteristically transcended Dwarf obsession for gold and jewels, and asked for nothing. He was rewarded with three strands of her golden hair as a sign of the renewed friendship between the two races along with the promise "that your hands will flow with gold, yet over you gold shall have no dominion."[144] A sign of the Dwarves subjection to the Dark Lord was their pride, lust for gold and possessiveness, which, given Gimli's love for Galadriel and her gift, will now potentially undergo transformation. Psychologically, they represent stubborn, prideful yet creative impulses and ability to work hard and produce beautiful physical objects.

Galadriel was an agent of Varda, also known as Elbereth, a name that means star-queen in Elf-Sindarin. The most powerful of the Female Valar, she had created the stars and set the star of hope, Eärendil, in the night sky. Both she and Galadriel show qualities similar to the Virgin Mary, as

---

[144] Tolkien, 2005b, p. 490

do other female figures of grace and beauty in *The Lord of the Rings* and *The Silmarillion*.[145] Galadriel's gift to Gimli bound his unfolding destiny to her through the three [3] strands of her golden hair and the magic of correspondence, which also related him to Varda, the feminine Force of Creation. Whereas Galadriel's hair represents her essential quality of being and, more specifically, her thoughts, qualitatively, the number Three [3] refers to dynamic process and insight. In fact, after the War of the Rings, Gimli became the link between Dwarves, Elves, Men and Ents, promising a more harmonious future for all races of Free People, which includes creative physical work in service to the divine Feminine and the unity of all life.

Dwarves were originally created prior to the two Children of Illúvatar, Elves, the Firstborn, and Men, the Second born. They were a creation of the smith-Valar, Aulë, in the depths of the earth, outside of the knowledge of Illúvatar, the One, and Aulë's spouse Yavanna, the Giver of Fruits and lover of all vegetation. According to Dwarf tradition, they were said to have descended from the Seven Dwarf Fathers who slept until the awakening of the Elves, at which time they also awoke. Despite their masculine origins, Aulë later reconciled his creation with Illúvatar, the One, as well as with Yavanna, indicating their fundamental relationship to the unity of the One and life, including vegetative life. Moreover, their home and workstation in the bowels of mountains that descend into the depths of the earth imply they were creative workers for the Great Earth Mother and the incarnated divine. Now that the Dwarves had re-gained a conscious and positive relationship to feminine spiritual light and Varda through the Elf-queen, Galadriel, their hard work, skill of craft, artistic sensibility and creativity can be used to help embody a higher spirit of unity, beauty and truth in Middle-earth. This possibility came hand in hand with the defeat of Sauron and his destructive forces of Evil, which dominated Middle-earth during the Third Age.

---

[145] Tolkien, 1981, p. 171-173 passim

INDIVIDUATION AND THE FOUR FUNCTIONS OF CONSCIOUSNESS

At another level, the goal of individuation is symbolized by the fact that the number of hobbits or halflings that set out on the quest total four (4), Frodo and Sam at the outset and Merry and Pippin shortly afterwards. To begin with, I believe it is safe to say that, as a group, they compensate for the collective consciousness at large, which was one-sidedly based on science and technology. As I indicated above, the Shire is divided into four [4] parts, suggesting that hobbits lived in a state of balanced wholeness, even if unconsciously.

The hobbits represent the natural religious person who lives in subjection to the Self in harmony with the earth and the animal soul, according to what Jung called "unconscious wholeness."[146] They bring, at least potentially, compensatory balance to life as a whole, much of which had been turned to evil purposes under the influence of Sauron. Their individuation reflects the potential for the coming Fourth Age, the Age of Man, to be lived in harmony and integrity.

In terms of psychological attitude, given the self-sufficiency of hobbits and their tendency not to travel but stay at home, they seem to have been more introverted than extraverted. In terms of the four [4] functions of consciousness, Frodo, the Ring-bearer represents the superior function, Sam, his loyal servant, the first auxiliary function, Merry, the older of the two younger hobbits, the second auxiliary function and Pippin, the youngest, the fourth and inferior function. Although their characteristics are somewhat sketchily described, it seems possible to attribute specific functions of consciousness to each of the four humble halflings.

FRODO AND THE SUPERIOR FUNCTION: INTUITION

It is likely that Frodo represents the intuitive function, given his primary openness to go on the quest and the fact that he willingly accepted the burden of the Ring without being aware of the way. He, in fact, grew

---

[146] As reported in Lawrence Jaffé, 1999, p. 59

increasingly self-reflective throughout the epic, a self-reflection based on his visionary goal of surrendering the Ring of Power, and the experience of the attractive allure of the counter-will of Sauron, in his form as the restless, ever-searching Eye of Sauron.

While in Lothlórien, he became the first of the four hobbits to recognize that he was part of a larger story, thanks to his intuitive vision in the mirror of Galadriel. Being aware of being part of a larger story means being conscious that one's life is connected to the archetypal substratum of existence and that it is not directed by the ego. Moreover he grew in maturity throughout the epic to the point that he seemed to have taken on Elven qualities and became a container for an inner light. In Shelob's lair, when he lay poisoned and unconscious, Sam observed that "Frodo's face was fair of hue again, pale but beautiful with an Elvish beauty, as of one who has long passed the shadows."[147] Earlier Sam had seen Frodo's care-worn and aged face emanating peace and lit by a light from within that shone "clearer and stronger" than ever.[148]

A different type, Sam consistently demonstrated his love and loyalty to Frodo and it becomes evident early on that Eros and feeling are always the determinative factor in his undertakings and moral choice. He is very conscious of both his likes and dislikes, which he did not hesitate to openly express. As much as he loved Frodo, Sam could not stand Gollum and his disgusting presence. When Frodo was poisoned, paralyzed and enveloped in the malevolent cords of Shelob in her dark and odious cave, he fought furiously against her, eventually penetrating the monster spider in the belly with Frodo's elven-sword, causing her a grievous wound.

He then remembered that he also had Frodo's gift from the Elf-queen, the Phial of Galadriel, which contained the light of Eärendil's star, a Silmaril, a jewel of brilliance, set in the sky as a sign of hope. With a spontaneous prayer to Elbereth, the star-queen, in the Elf-Sindarin language of the High Elves, which he did not consciously know, Sam gained courage and flashed the white light of Creation at the terrible

---

[147] Tolkien, 2005b, p. 959
[148] Ibid, p. 397

monster, which turned away in dire agony. This heart-felt invocation translated into English reads as: "O Elbereth Starkindler from heaven gazing afar, to thee I cry now in the shadow of death. O look towards me, Everwhite."[149] This beautiful prayer, spoken in a High Elvin language of differentiated Eros and feeling, comes to Sam thanks not only to his critical and traumatic circumstances, but also to his open and loving heart.

SAM AND THE FIRST AUXILLIARY FUNCTION: FEELING

Sam represents the feeling function, the function of consciousness that, when grounded in Eros, has the readiest access to the incarnated soul and psychic being. As Galadriel had promised, the phial was a light in a dark place, "when all the other lights go out."[150] Sam had accessed the psychic being's light of truth, which alone could dispel the surrounding darkness and evil of Shelob, the horrible devouring monster. Inasmuch as the Elf language was foreign to him, he is only beginning to relate to this deeper aspect of his psyche, which is essential for an integral transformation of being.

In Sermon VII of Jung's early work, *Septem Sermones ad Mortuous [Seven Sermons to the Dead]*, which he first published privately, he wrote: "This Star is the god and goal of man/ ....To this one god man shall pray/ Prayer increaseth the light of the Star. It casteth a bridge over death. It prepareth life for the smaller world and assuageth the hopeless desires of the greater."[151] Here Jung is saying that not only will assessing one's inner star light up the darkness of being, even of death, but that conscious individuation directs life towards the small, apparently insignificant or rejected aspects of life, for purposes of assimilation and wholeness. In this regard, it is particularly noteworthy that Tolkien elevated the small in his epic in his choice of a hobbit to be the Ring-bearer, and the high respect he gave to all the four hobbits involved in the quest. In a private interview

---

[149] Peter J. Kreeft, 2005, p. 76
[150] Tolkien, 2005a, p. 491
[151] 1965, p. 389

he recounted that the hobbits "were made small in size because it reflects the generally small reach of their imagination – not the small reach of their courage or latent power."[152]

In Jung's sermon, the star clearly refers to the quintessence and centre of the incarnated individual being, what Sri Aurobindo and the Mother called the psychic being. The latter two especially emphasized the need for the primacy of the psychic transformation and individualization for the sake of a centered wholeness, prior to engaging in a more far-reaching spiritual transformation.[153] The path always requires honoring the small, which is similar to the New Testament injunction that the first will be last and the last will be first.

MERRY AND THE SECOND AUXILLIARY FUNCTION: THINKING

Merry was immature at the beginning and for some time during the epic, but, along with Pippin, matures to the point of receiving a knighthood. Throughout the epic he was depicted as cautious, studious and curious, telling signs of a budding mental orientation towards life. He also proved himself courageous and capable when he, along with Éowyn, a beautiful shield-maiden, slew the Lord of the Nazgûls during the Battle of the Pelennor [Elf-Sindarin: 'fenced land'] Fields.[154] His participation in slaying the Demon, which he did with an Elf-blade, means that he had gained some Elf discernment, which he used to discriminate the nature of this perverted Evil dynamism. Under Aragorn's instructions that Merry be "armed for battle," the warrior woman dressed Merry in armor of the knights of Rohan, emblazoned with a picture of a white horse.[155] Gandalf also encouraged Merry to live up to his natural potential, which was still somewhat unconscious. His new found relationship with Éowyn, a brave and valorous anima figure, opened him up to realize his natural courageous

---

[152] As reported in Joseph Pearce, 1998, p. 153
[153] A. S. Dalal, 2002
[154] Tolkien, 2005c
[155] Ibid, p. 1049

self and warrior spirit, a spirit that was carried by instinctually pure libido, symbolized by the white horse.

Merry was later healed by Aragorn in a House of Healing, using *athelas* [Elf-Sindarin: 'kingsfoil'], after he nearly died from the Black Breath. His healing suggests that Merry had assimilated a considerable amount of kingly courage and right consciousness, and the ability to confront the spirit of fear, embodied in the terrible Lord of the Nazgûls. It also suggests he recognized Aragorn as rightful King with healing hands, capable of bringing healing to the people and a renewed consciousness of truth.

Merry was rewarded for his valor and made a knight of Rohan. Back in the Shire he was a leader for the Hobbit forces in the Battle of Bywater, and later became Master of Buckland and a Counselor of the North-Kingdom. Thanks to the likes of Merry and Pippin, and no doubt Sam, and their integration of shadow and maturation into their higher nature, the Hobbits could now defend themselves against evil incursions. Merry represents the third function of thinking, which may have been reflected in these latter two positions, but is more precisely indicated by his natural studious inclinations and the fact that he was recorded as having written several scholarly books (Robert Foster, 1978). Although he represents the thinking function, his scholarship no doubt includes the courage of conviction and search for truth that Merry's warrior spirit imparted.

PIPPIN AND THE INFERIOR FUNCTION: SENSATION

Pippin, the youngest hobbit to go on the quest, represents the undeveloped inferior function, sensation. Throughout the story he was depicted as having the most mundane concerns such as a good meal, finding an Inn to have some ale and having a good night's sleep, which is typical of someone with a developing sensation function. His inferior status was portrayed by the fact that he was the most immature of the members of the fellowship. As is typical of the inferior function, which is the portal for both good and evil due to its lack of differentiation, Pippin, was the one that revealed himself to Sauron the Black sorcerer, after foolishly stealing the *palantír* [Elf-Quenya: 'far-seer'], the seeing-stone, from the sleeping Gandalf, knowing full well that he was doing wrong [156]. Earlier on, in the Mines of Moria, it was also Pippin who, out of idle curiosity, ill-advisedly dropped a stone into a deep well that alerted the terrible Balrog of the existence of the intruding Fellowship.[157]

He and Merry were captured by Orcs at Parth Galen [Elf-Sindarin] and later escaped, when he managed to loosen his binding cords and cut his way free using a black Orc-knife, suggesting some shadow discernment, specifically of the nature of disharmonious driveness. Earlier he had the presence of mind to let his elven-broach drop on the trail to Isengard [Rohan: 'iron-enclosure'], where they were being carried by Orcs, with the possibility that members of the Fellowship would find it and become aware of their whereabouts (Tolkien, 2005b). Not only did Pippin let go of any attachment to this spiritual gift, a sign of maturation, the broach was later found by Aragorn, alerting him, Legolas and Gimli to the fact they were still alive, encouraging their search. The inferior function is not only clumsy and foolish, but open to innovative possibilities that are closed to the more conventional and well-ordered superior functions.

Characteristic of the inferior function, Pippin hastily and without reflection offered his services with a flourish to Denethor [Elf-Sindarin: '-eagle'], the Chief Steward of Gondor, painting a gallant picture of himself in the process. Denethor accepted, perhaps more to serve his own purposes than anything else, which was to discover how his son, Baromir was slain, as well as surrounding events and personalities. Pippin, however, later became aware of his madness, and had gained the maturity and independence of being to break his sworn allegiance, and help to save Faramir, his other son's, life.[158] He also showed his valor in marching with the Army of the West to the Morannon (Elf-Sindarin; 'black-gate') and slayed a great troll.

After the War of the Rings, Pippin was made a Knight of Gondor

---

[156] Tolkien, 2005b
[157] Tolkien, 2005a
[158] Tolkien, 2005c

and King's messenger, and returned to the Shire to help mobilize the Hobbits against the Chief's men, who were course, ugly and offensive, while imposing an exploitive, destructive and oppressive Rule on the Shire and elsewhere, since the four hobbits left on their quest.[159] He found fulfillment in his higher law of being as a chivalrous knight, although not a thinker like Merry, but simply a man of action and sensation type intrinsically involved in the joy and sorrow of life, the dynamic reality of the give and take of engagement. One can imagine that, with age, his taste buds and palate became increasingly refined. During the course of the quest and later, Pippin, too, became more mature, having integrated a considerable amount of shadow as well as the light of discernment and capacity to make moral choices for the good.

In addition to the kingsfoil administered to Merry by Aragorn, there were three types of special medicines and nourishment imbibed by both Merry and Pippin during their journey, each with its own value. To begin with they were nourished by the Elf soul-food and way bread, *lembas*, which had the effect of giving them a wholesome feeling and a hopeful heart. The two young hobbits, in other words, were able to assimilate the positive virtues and light of the Elves, which helped them on their inner journey.

Merry had a gash on his forehead that was cured with a dark Orc ointment. He and Pippin, both exhausted from their ordeal with the Orcs, were also forced to imbibe some burning Orc liquid, which gave them strength to stand up and carry on, and feel very much alive. Thus, the two hobbits were also capable of integrating some invigorating shadow values, which helped them gain endurance for the journey.

Finally, Merry and Pippin were given Ent-draughts to drink by the oldest Ent, Fangorn also known as Treebeard, for refreshment and nourishment while they were convalescing in the Forest of Fangorn after escaping the Orcs. Because of this, both Merry and Pippin eventually grew to four and one half feet tall, the tallest of Hobbits. The suggestion is that imbibing the liquid brought a form of healing that allowed the two hobbits

---

[159] Ibid.

to connect to the psychosomatic psyche and the autonomous nervous system in a healthy way, making them particularly robust, with a more open and enlarged imagination than the normal hobbit. Individuation and differentiation of being is indicated in *The Lord of the Rings* by the transformation indicated by each of the four hobbits including the two youngest, both of whom who grew into maturity and honor.

INDIVIDUATION OF THE FOUR SOUL-TYPES

THE SOUL-TYPE OF THE PRIEST AND MAGUS

Gandalf was an Istari, known to the Elves as Mithrandir [Elf-Sindarin: 'grey-pilgrim'], and he represents the priestly soul-type and magus. He was an incarnated lesser Valar [power of the One] and emissary of the primary Valar and feminine Creatrix, Varda also known as Elbereth, the star-Queen, and charged, along with his fellow Istari, to care for Varda, the earth and the Free People. He wore a wide-brimmed hat and a cloak, had a grey beard and always carried a staff, representing his spiritual authority and function as a *hermeneutic* guide. He was a wayfarer, appearing throughout Middle-earth, had shamanic powers, was associated with eagles and was the chief organizer of the war against Sauron. He also had an irascible side and was considered by his enemy and others to initiate trouble and strife. In both his physical appearance and many of his attributes and associated eagle spirit, he resembled the primary Norse god, Odin or Wotan.[160] The eagle spirit, common to both Wotan and Gandalf, points to spiritual vision and nobility, along with power and cruelty and the instinct of the predator. Gandalf initiated the quest to surrender the Ring of Power, the inner nature of which is evident in the fact of the many reported dreams and archetypal visions in the story especially by Frodo, but also by Baromir, Sam, Aragorn and Pippin.

It is highly interesting that Jung had a similar guiding figure he called Philemon, with whom he had an inner dialogue, coming to him both in

---

[160] Marjorie Burns, 2005

dreams and in active imagination, an actively engaged meditative process. He said, that Philemon taught him about the objectivity and reality of the psyche, giving him teachings that lead to psychological freedom. Jung described him as a "pagan [who] brought with him an Egypto-Hellenistic atmosphere with a Gnostic coloration."[161] In Jung's vision, Philemon was an old man with the horns of a bull and came holding a set of four [4] keys, suggesting he held the keys to knowledge of the Self and wholeness. According to Jung, he represented superior insight and the spiritual aspect and meaning of life. In this way he resembles Indra, the Vedic bull-god of illumined thought, who brought psychological knowledge to humankind, showing the individual the right way of acting, with its attendant feelings of *Ananda* [bliss].[162]

Philemon, likewise, had characteristics that are attributed to the angel Metraton, who was a guide for the biblical patriarch, Enoch.[163] In addition to Enoch, Elijah and John the Baptist are, according to legend, considered to be embodiments of Metraton, relating them to Philemon. In fact, in Jung's visions, Philemon developed out of an earlier Elijah figure. Merlin of the Arthurian Cycle also had characteristics similar to Elijah, both of whom were depicted as hairy, as was John the Baptist. Their hairiness suggests integration of the instinctual psyche. Despite his similarities to Wotan, Gandalf was also described with many qualities that remind one of Merlin, and he played the same role as the latter as *hermeneutic* guide to knights on a quest. Moreover, Merlin renounced worldly power like Gandalf, who renounced ambition for spiritual and political dominion. Inasmuch as he was a leader of the Free People, and an agent of the One, Gandalf was also similar to Moses, the prophet and guide to freedom of the Jewish people. Fleming Rutledge, however, believes that he was more akin to Elijah than Moses, in that he did battle with archetypal forces of evil, "the principalities and powers."[164] Philemon represents superior

---

[161] 1965, p. 182

[162] Dr. Soumitra Basu, Dr. A. K. Basu, 2002

[163] Marie-Louise von Franz, 1975

[164] 2004, p. 187

knowledge and meaning, just as does Gandalf, especially later in the story after his battle with the Balrog and transfiguration into Gandalf the White. The similarity of Gandalf to Philemon becomes readily apparent when one knows that Gandalf's Elven name was *Olórin*, where *Olor* is a Quenya-Elf word meaning dream, not of the ordinary kind, but an archetypal dream or fantasy from the objective psyche.[165]

Gandalf's refusal to join Saruman, the rebel Istari, who tempted him to join the latter in his quest for dominion through Knowledge, Rule, Order, the same design, but using different means than that employed by the freedom loving White Council, speaks to Gandalf's loyalty to Varda and his spiritual purpose on Middle-earth. In his debate with Sauruman, who promoted self-righteous pride and control over others, the sincerity of his conscious intent was put to the test. Here he rejected the possibility of seemingly doing good by foul means through the use of deceit and the domination of others, Sauruman's strategy and ambition. Previously, he had rejected the Ring of Power offered to him by Frodo at the council of Elrond in Lórien, exclaiming that it was too dangerous for him to take it as he recognized he was easily tempted by pity for weakness and ambition for power to do good. His transformation from Gandalf the Grey to Gandalf the White involved battling with the Balrog, a fallen Maiar, and spirit of terror and destruction, hatred and long-smoldering anger in service to Sauron.[166] The dreadful struggle involved a terrifying descent from the bridge of Khaza-dûn in the Mines of Moria to the cold waters of the abyss and death, to the heights of the white Silvertine mountains known by the Dwarves as Zirak-Zigal [Dwarf-Khuzdhul], one of the three mountains of Moria and the *Axis Mundi*, the centre of the world. There, he was finally able to send the Balrog smashing to the side of the mountain below. Gandalf had not only refused the intoxication of power domination in conscious intent but he struggled mightily to raise to consciousness, on Mount Silvertine, the nature of the demon of the perverted power instinct and rejected it as well. Gandalf's transfiguration is based on the same

---

[165] Verlyn Flieger,1997
[166] Tolkien, 2005a, 2005b

archetypal pattern depicted in Christ's temptation and rejection of power as well as his decent into hell and resurrection.

His healing involved both a return to the beginning of creation and time, where his cloak, hair and beard metamorphosed from grey to white and, later, a stay at the Elf-haven, Lórien, where he was born by Gwaihir (Elf-Sindarin: 'wind-lord') the WIndlord, the Lord of Eagles of the Misty Mountains. Healing involved, first, understanding the meaning of his struggle with the evil Demon, as symbolized by being carried by the noble and far-seeing eagle, then rest and soul-assimilation outside of time in Lórien. By rejecting the Balrog shadow, Gandalf not only gained in power and endurance but he became invulnerable to weapons or any perverted impulses, self-righteous angers, lack of sympathy, or divisive hatreds that aim at destroying his purity of intent.

His vehicle, Shadowfax, one of the greatest of the Rohan [Elf-Sindarin: 'horse-land'] steeds, on whom Gandalf rode like the blowing wind, as if they were one, points to the instinctual purity of his dynamic intent.[167] Before Gandalf took him, he was required to tame him as he had never been previously mounted, indicating the need to civilize powerful natural instincts.[168] Indeed, his name, Shadowfax, also suggests Gandalf's capacity to have related to and assimilated invigorating shadow dynamism. It is indicative of the fact that despite his spiritual status as a Maiar and other-worldliness, he was very concerned with and involved in the galloping hooves of unfolding of time and the formation of culture.

Given his purity of heart and instinctual libido, reflected by his whiteness and the spiritual essence of *fana*, the inner light of the Valar that permeated his being, his energy could now be fully directed to the victory over evil.[169] The fact that the word *fanturi*, with its root in *fana*, refers to visions and dreams, suggests that there was now a purified and direct connection to the archetypal psyche and that Gandalf the White's

---

[167] Tolkien, 2005b

[168] Tolkien 2005a

[169] Timothy R. O'Neil, 1979

power of healing and redemption had been amplified.[170] His wholeness of being is indicated in the fact that, in addition to his main soul-type as a priest, he embodied the essence of the other three soul-types; he was an energetic leader and organizer; he was at ease and related to his fellow common person; and he was servant to both Varda, the power of Creation, and all the Free People of Middle-earth.

THE SOUL-TYPE OF THE LEADER AND KING

The second hero figure, Aragorn, represents the soul-type of the leader and King, with its associated natural ethical and spiritual values and instincts. His transformation and growing maturity began with his professed lack of interest in taking the Ring of Power from Frodo early on in the story at the Prancing Pony Inn at Bree, when he first met Frodo and the other three hobbits. As he observed to the hobbits in informing them that he was a friend of Gandalf and that he was Aragorn son of Arathorn, "If I was after the Ring I could have it - Now."[171] After that display of strength he then humbly stated to the mistrustful hobbits that "if by life or death I can save you I will," exhibiting a noble spirit and instinct for self-sacrifice.[172] Later in Lórien, during the council of Elrond, Frodo offered him the Ring of Power as the rightful heir, since his ancestor Isildur (Elf-Quenya: 'moon') severed the finger of Sauron along with the Ring, although it then got lost. Aragorn's measured response was "it does not belong to either of us .... but it has been ordained that you should hold it for awhile."[173] In other words, he did not seek unlawful power and dominion over others, even though he understood his destiny was to be the future King of Gondor, only that people find their right place in life.

It is noteworthy that his noble attitude contrasted from another courageous leader, a leading Captain of Gondor, Baromir, who, through

---

[170] Verilyn Flieger, 1997
[171] Tolkien, 2005a, p. 224
[172] Ibid.
[173] Ibid, p. 321

pride, lusted after the Ring of Power tempted to do what he believed to be good for his people. As I recounted above, he attempted to obtain the Ring from Frodo, using this potentially compelling argument. The end result was Frodo's slipping on the Ring to escape Baromir's insistence, and the latter eventually being attacked and killed by the black arrows of the Orcs. Psychologically, this means that Baromir was poisoned by arrows of anger and hatred, which caused disunity to the Fellowship of the Ring. While he lay there dying, however, he confessed his sin to Aragorn, acknowledging him as his King and received his absolution and blessings.

Aragorn initially presented himself as Strider, a homely-looking Ranger who patrolled the Shire and elsewhere from the encroaching darkness and the Black Riders, also known as Ringwraiths or Nazgûls, who were drawn by lust for the Ring. He later declared himself to be Aragorn son of Arathorn, the future King of Gondor. Throughout the story, he increasingly revealed himself as Aragorn, the son of Arathorn, whose father-line descended directly from Isildur, Elendil's (Elf-Quenya: 'star-lover' or 'elf-friend') son of Minas Ithil (Elf-Sindarin: 'tower of the moon'); he was therefore the rightful heir to Gondor's throne of which Elendil was the first founder.[174] Yet, when he was offered the Ring of Power by Frodo, based on the fact that his ancestor Isildur had initially obtained the Ring by cutting off Sauron's finger, he refused, stating that the Ring belonged to nobody. Isildur lost the Ring as it slipped from his finger, and he was slain by one of Sauron's Orcs. The reigning monarch being killed by one of Sauron's Orcs, psychologically, suggests that fear and Orc-like impulses of impatience, dissension, mistrust, cruelty and disunity took over Gondor and Middle-earth, along with the ascendancy of the destructive spirit of Sauron.

The Ring eventually found its way to Gollum who was possessed by it for some 478 years until he lost it to Bilbo, who eventually bequeathed it to Frodo, initiating the quest of *The Lord of the Rings*.[175] Aragorn declared that his task was to rectify "Isildur's fault," and labor unendingly to undo

---

[174] Paul H. Kocker, 1972
[175] Robert Foster, 1978

ancestral karma."[176] Isildur's wrong involved his acceding to the temptation to the Ring of Power although, at the same time, he inadvertently opened up the possibility of its eventual unmaking. Aragorn was brought up in Rivendell by Elrond, who educated him with the wisdom of the Elves, helping to prepare him to redeem his ancestral sin, which involved not only rejecting the arrogant claim to power and dominion over others like Sauron, but also the narrow impulses of hatred, cruelty, and drive to disunity of the Orcs, who were made in mockery of the Elves. If the Balrog is specifically Gandalf the Maiar's demonic shadow of terror, then the Orc represents the Elf-educated Aragorn's specific black demon of hatred and disunity.

Throughout the epic, Aragorn gained in maturity and self-definition as king and rightful heir to the throne of Gondor, showing that he possessed leadership, nobility, courage, the spirit of self-sacrifice, righteousness, justice, mercy, forgiveness, creativity, foresight, wisdom, the healing touch and other Elf-like soul sensibilities. In fact Aragorn manifested considerable wholeness of being. In addition to his main soul-type as a leader, he embodied the essence of the other three soul-types; he fulfilled the priestly function as a man of knowledge and as a healer; he was at ease and related to his fellow common person, first as Strider, then as Aragorn; and, as King, he became servant to all his subjects as well as Manwë, the mightiest power for Good of the One, representing him on Middle-earth.

A significant moment transpired with the re-forging of Elendil's sword by the Elf-smiths at Rivendell, fulfilling an ancient prophecy that when the Ring was found, the sword that was shattered in a fight between Elendil and Sauron, would be re-forged.[177] Previously Aragorn only possessed the hilt of Elendil's sword, Narsil [Elf-Quenya: 'sun-moon'], which was presented to him by Elrond when he came of age. With its re-integration with the blade, it became Anduril, [Elf-Quenya: 'west-brilliance"], once broken, now a symbol of kingly integrity and authority, invested with ancient powers of relational involvement, discernment, and justice.

176

177 Ibid

Galadriel's parting gift to Aragorn, as he was preparing to leave Lórien, was a sheath for his sword, overlaid with a design of silver and gold flowers and leaves, along with elven-runes in gems spelling the name of the sword, Anduril, and recounting its lineage.[178] This gift ensured that Anduril would never be stained or broken if drawn from the sheath. The psychological implication is that, as long as the sword of leadership is contained in Elf-feeling and Eros values and visionary sensibilities, Aragorn will make pure and stainless decisions.

A second parting gift that Aragorn held dear to his heart, and which he pinned to his breast, was a beautiful silver broach containing the "Elfstone of the House of Elendil."[179] This gem bound him directly to Arwen Evenstar, his bethrothed, future spouse and Queen, and her elven lineage, which included her father, Elrond, Lord of Rivendell for whom she was the only daughter, and Galadriel, the Lady of Lórien and Celeborn (Elf Sindarin: (tall) 'silver tree') the Wise, Lord of Lórien, having kinship with the Elves of Lothlórien through her mother.[180] This gift seems to have portended that Aragorn's ordained destiny involved a growing conscious soul-centered relationship to Elf sensibilities and knowledge, as indicated in the fact that he was henceforth also named Elessar, the Elfstone, and eventually King Elessar.[181]

An important step in regaining his place as King was for Aragorn to demonstrate his capacity as a healer.[182] In the words of "Loreth [Elf-Sindarin], wise woman of Gondor: *The hands of the king are the hands of a healer, and so shall the rightful king be known.*"[183] With the help of the herbal mixture of *atheles,* known by the peasants as kingsfoil, he was able to bring healing to Faramir, noble Captain of Gondor, Éowyn, the courageous shield-maiden of Rohan, eventually Faramir's spouse and

---

[178] Tolkien. 2005a
[179] Ibid p. 489
[180] Tolkien, 2005c
[181] Ibid.
[182] Ibid.
[183] Ibid, p. 1129

Merry, the hobbit.[184] They all suffered from a dangerous dose of the hideous Black Breath in their fight against the dark forces of Evil during the War of the Pelennor Fields. Faramir also suffered a superficial wound from a Southron arrow as well as weariness and grief over his father, Denethor's madness and mood of pride and despair.[185] Psychologically, this means that all of the three sick people had assimilated spiritual values and enhanced courage to the face of the spirit of negation and fear. For one thing, It involved accepting their ordained place in life, Faramir as Steward of Gondor, Éowyn as his spouse and Merry as a Knight of Gondor. Faramir had to give up any claims to kingship, Éowyn her longing for the heart of Aragorn and Merry had to grow into the higher ethical and spiritual law of his being as a knight and warrior for truth. Accepting Aragorn's kingly authority and his consciousness and vision of life for the renewed Kingdom is an essential aspect of everybody finding their right place in life. As King, he was destined to not only bring healing to leading individuals but to the people as a whole and their way of life.

Another milestone in Aragorn's growing individuation as king came when he revealed himself by way of the *palentír* of Orthanc [Elf-Sindarin: 'forked height'] to Sauron as Elendil's heir, rightful ruler of Gondor.[186][187] Thus, he boldly declared himself to be a king with the integrity, authority, courage and creative capacity to conquer Sauron and his destructive spirit. It also served the tactical purpose of distracting Sauron from Frodo's quest to destroy the Ring in the Fire of Doom. His earlier fearless entry into the land of the Dead and freeing the Wraiths of Dunharrow, who died not having fulfilled their oaths of ages long past to fight against the Dark Lord, was an act of courage that helped to restore order and balance in the kingdom.[188] Bringing harmony to life requires cultures to resolve collective *karma*, the "sins of the fathers" which, according biblical reference, visit

---

[184] Ibid.
[185] Tolkien, 2005c
[186] Paul H. Kocker, 1972
[187] Tolkien, 2005c
[188] Tolkien, 2005c

us for three or four generations.[189] Psychologically, this involves the conscious recognition and resolution by individuals of family *karma* and/or burdensome *karma* from other times and other lives. It involves secular and spiritual leaders of countries to recognize and to work towards resolving past collective *karma*.

The final act of Aragorn's assuming the mantle of King began when he repeated Elendil's ritual promise on arriving from Númenor in Elvish, that "in this place will I abide, and my heirs, unto the ending of the world." His reference to Elendil, the "First Ancestor-Founding King," and the numinous "first times of the first beginnings" is a ritual recollection of the original heroic accomplishments, potency and life-giving ideals of his people.[190] Given the lyrical and enduring quality of the Elf language, this was a strong commitment to rule according to the highest Númenorean tradition, coming straight from Aragorn's soul.[191] He was now invested with all the duties and responsibilities of the King of the Re-united Kingdoms, consummated by being crowned by Gandalf, to whom he humbly acknowledged that the victory against the forces of darkness belonged. In fact, it was Gandalf, who represents superior insight and connection to inner worlds, who initiated the quest for individuation and coming to terms with the Shadow; and he was the chief *hermeneutic* guide throughout.

Aragorn also acknowledged the important and integral role of Frodo the Ring-bearer by having him pass the crown to Gandalf. Earlier, great praise was accorded to both Frodo and Sam by the men of Gondor. There was also recognition of the beginning of a legend involving Frodo [and Sam] when a minstrel of Gondor announced that he would sing to the Free People of the West a lay "of Frodo of the Nine Fingers and the Ring of Doom.[192]" Finally all four hobbits were honored by Aragorn on their departure from Ithilien (Elf-Sindarin: Moon land or 'Land

---

[189] Exodus 20:5, 6; Numbers 14: 18; Deuteronomy 5:9, 10
[190] John Weir Perry, 1970, p. 22
[191] Paul H. Kocker, 1972, p. 149
[192] Tolkien, 2005c, p. 1249

of Silvery Moonlight') and "arrayed as princes of the land."[193] In their individuation and growing maturity, the victory was also theirs. They represent the common person in touch with the earth, the only beings humble enough to risk the adventure of the Ring. Their recognition by Aragorn acknowledged the importance of the integrity of common people to the development of a balanced and harmonious society. The influence and moral responsibility of common folk to the well-being of culture, for better or for worse, is becoming increasingly evident in our times with the internet and reality TV. Psychologically, each hobbit represents a different function of consciousness that became increasingly differentiated throughout the epic.

Aragorn's human personality now became transparent to the archetype of the King and Arwen the beautiful Elf-maid came to him as Queen. Complete Individuation of the King requires highly differentiated Eros and feeling values, which the Queen represents, connecting the King and his decisions to the people and the land. Arwen brought with her all the soulful sensibilities and farsightedness of the Elven race and Aragorn had often shown the capacity to move gracefully in the world of both Men and of Elves. He had, in fact, fulfilled the image of the victorious Christ, cultural healer and Lord of both the Living and the Dead.

His marriage to Arwen portends a fruitful and just rule in the coming Fourth Age of Man. The sacred marriage of the King and Queen is a symbolic physical enactment of the *hierosgamos* of the Father God and Mother Goddess, and representation of the harmonious balance of masculine and feminine energies of the Self. In Tolkien's cosmology, as king, Aragorn was the earthly representative of Manwë [Elf-Quenya: 'good, pure'], the noblest offspring of the Mind of Illúvatar, who best understood his will and thought; and as queen, Arwen was the earthly representative of Manwë's spouse, Varda, the exalted, the latter's power of creation. King Aragorn, whose destiny was reflected in his name, which means royal tree, represents the ruling consciousness, which is now in balance and harmony. As King Elessar, the Elfstone, he was directly related to the Elves and

---

[193] ibid, p. 1276

their cultural heritage through his spouse, and that will directly inform his kingship. Queen Arwen, whose name, which means royal maiden, reflecting her high destiny, symbolizes ruling Eros and feeling values that promote love, fellowship, community and reverence for all life. Their future off-springs will represent new creative life potential given the new ruling consciousness and values. In his role as King, Aragorn not only plays the role of protector of the people, for which he has ample front-line experience, but, along with Queen Arwen, he is also the bringer of order and giver of life, where individual lives are potentially tied harmoniously to the cosmic order. Psychologically, this refers to the possibility for individuals to now internalize and live in conscious harmony with the values and attitudes embodied by King Aragorn and Queen Arwen, along with the creative potential life now brings.

To complete the symbolic meaning of the renewal in consciousness and life that is taking place, the Withered Tree in the courtyard of Minas Tirith, formerly a White Tree burned by Sauron, was replaced by a sapling of the White Tree, found by Gandalf near the snowline of the Mindolluin [Elf-Sindarin: 'towering-head-blue'] mountain.[194] The tree had dark leaves above and silver leaves below, with clusters of flowers. The new tree is expected to bloom and to foster the growth of new saplings. The White Tree has a lineage that dated back to the original first created tree at the beginning of time. It had roots that go back to the original light of creation and the Imperishable Fire. Its white and silver color indicates purity and lunar receptivity, while the symbol of the tree refers to individuation and unfolding life, life that is firmly rooted in the essence of being. Its flowers represent soul values and spiritual aspiration. The dark leaves above point to spiritual potential that still lies in the unconscious. This is an exceptionally poignant image of healing for individuals and our present culture that holds little respect for historical roots, one that seems to sunder its connection to the past in every generation. It is important to be rooted in the soil of history while allowing for the evolutionary development of consciousness and individuation.

---

[194] Tolkien, 2005C

THE SOUL-TYPE OF THE TRADER AND QUEST HERO

The bearer of the Ring of Power, Frodo, represents a third soul-type, that of the common man and trader. The Ring is the central focus of the epic and it was Frodo's task to destroy it by throwing it in the Fire of Doom burning at the heart of the Crack of Doom. After extreme trial and suffering, Frodo managed to do that through an act of grace, making him by the end of the quest a highly individuated, although, as is typically the case, a flawed hero. As a common man living in close harmony with the earth and the animal soul, Frodo's natural instincts were to stay close to home. But Gandalf drew him onto a quest to take on and surrender the Ring of Power, something he believed only a hobbit could do, because of their relative innocence. In psychological terms, leaving home on a quest can be understood as a *felix culpa*, a violation against nature for the sake of increasing consciousness and individuation.

The quest, which puts the principle focus on the need to surrender the Ring of Power for the sake of truth and justice in the regulation of life, drew together both light and dark forces. I think it is fair to argue that the Ring of Power itself, being the central factor in the epic, is the magnet that drew together both the elements of good and those of evil. Moreover, as becomes clear throughout the story, more consciousness of the shadow, the spirits and demons of evil, always induces a purifying transformation of being and integration of personality. This was no less the case with Frodo as it is with the other heroic figures in the drama. Frodo's first encounter with evil began at the outset and culminated at a sheltered dell at the foot of Weathertop at the summit of which were the remnants of a watch tower, the Tower of Amon Sûl [Elf-Sindarin: 'hill of the wind'].[195] There, in the dell, the Lord of the Nazgûls, the leader of the Ringwraiths or Black Riders, high servants of Sauron, inflicted a painful wound on his shoulder by the shard of a Morgul-knive, enchanted with black powers. Gandalf later informed Frodo that the splinter from the Morgul-knife was

---

[195] Tolkien, 2005a

working its way to his heart, but that he was healed in time.[196] By wearing the Ring, Frodo became invisible to the normal world of Middle-earth but was, at the same time, drawn into the dark world of Sauron and other dark forces. Not only could he see the Nazgûls, who are normally invisible, only recognized by their black clothes, but they could see him.

The Nazgûls were originally men who were enslaved by the nine Rings given to mortal men and were possessed by dominion and power; they worked as Sauron's messengers and scouts and were inexorably drawn to the One ruling Ring. They were particularly potent at night and in deserted places, emitted loud, piercing cries, and instilled terror in their victims. The fact that Frodo saw the Nazgûls indicates that he was beginning to become conscious of the dangers involved in being the Ring-bearer and the dispiriting effect of the Ringwraith shadow and its black spirit of fear. Since Frodo, in turn, became more visible to the shadow world, more conscious to inner forces of negation, psychologically suggests that a mobilization of hostile inner voices will persist in discouraging him on his quest for conscious individuation and truth. His becoming invisible to normal sight means the nature of the shadow is incomprehensible to normal consciousness.

Had the knife-shard worked its way to his heart, Frodo would have become a lesser Ringwraith, under the dominion of the Nazgûls. In other words, he would have become individualistic, proud, and driven by power and dominion over others in personal relationships and at the local level of the community, a defense against fear. This typically plays itself out in power games and prestige concerns, involvement in intrigues, critical, and poisonous remarks, undermining and repressing healthy ideas, opinions and activities, insinuations to and about others, and the use of knowledge for selfish ends, in order to hurt or diminish others, along with the establishment of one's superiority. Frodo was eventually healed at the Elf-haven, Rivendell, after a long rest. However, the burden of carrying the Ring and the suffering and dangers to one's psychic equilibrium it entailed was beginning to become self-evident. Because of his encounter

---

[196] Ibid

with the Shadow, his wound and eventual healing, presumably involving overcoming both his fear and propensity to have dominion over others, Frodo gained in transparency and openness to truth. As Gandalf observed there was a hint of transparency in the convalescing Frodo, then mused to himself: "He may become like a glass filled with a clear light for eyes to see that can."[197]

Frodo eventually became conscious of Gollum/Sméagol [Old-English: 'burrowing, worming in'], who was a hobbit, although disfigured and perverted from many years of possessing the Ring of Power.[198] Inasmuch as Frodo represents the humble common man and trader on a lonely journey to find his unique individual personality, Gollum represents the shadow side of the common man who can be mean and narrow-minded, hateful, spiteful, nasty, treacherous and isolated. His covetous and hateful inclination, even early on in his very long life, was apparent in that he had killed his cousin Déagol [Old English: 'secret'], who had initially found the Ring, in order to possess it himself. As Gollum, he had become a despicable creature, not only in appearance but in mentality. He feared all things Elven, hated every creature, was nasty, spiteful and treacherous, and yet expressed a pitiful cringing and fawning behavior towards his master Frodo, possibly in an effort to become free of the Ring.

Despite his defective character, Gollum served an essential role in leading the hobbits, Frodo and Sam, to Cirith Ungol, the least guarded route into Mordor, partly out of fear of Frodo, the Ring-bearer, and partly to ensure that Sauron did not retrieve the Ring.[199] Gollum's inner confusion, his lack of clarity of purpose, his own passionate desire for the Ring, and his distaste for light, both physical and spiritual, his isolation from creaturely warmth, and yet the reality of a small part of him that was open to good, all played a role in inducing him to act as a guide for Frodo in order to help him fulfill his task. Since the taming of Sméagol prior to the journey through the Dead Marshes, Gollum was depicted as divided

---

[197] Tolkien, 2005a, p. 291
[198] Tolkien, 2005b
[199] Tolkien. 2005b, 2005c

against himself, the potentially good aspect represented by his Sméagol personality, his alter-ego, and his more evil inclinations as the more obsessed and willful Gollum with whom he more consciously identified.[200] Psychologically, Gollum represents the humanly isolated, narrow-minded, nasty, spiteful and possessive aspect of Frodo, the common man, which shuns truth and is fearful of being exposed to the light of consciousness. Not rejecting the Gollum shadow kept Frodo humble and allowed him to pursue his goal of surrendering the Ring of Power, not only for his own sake, but for the sake of all the Free People of Middle-earth.

It kept him humble that is, until the decisive moment at the Crack of Doom when he could fulfill his purpose and surrender the Ring to the Fire. Rather than surrendering the Ring, Frodo was, instead, seized with an inexorable passion to possess the Ring. He did not throw it in, initiating a struggle with Gollum, which came to a climax with the latter biting off the third finger of Frodo's right hand, along with the Ring. The dramatic struggle culminated in Gollum falling into the Fire of Doom along with the Ring of Power. He was, in other words, consumed by the fire that fueled his desire for power and malicious intent. This event eventuated success of the mission, the unmaking of the Ring and the downfall of Sauron and the Dark Forces.

Although the end signaled a defeat of Frodo's conscious will, Tolkien described the event as an act of grace, "the unforeseeable result of free action of Frodo, Gollum and Sam."[201] Psychologically, Frodo, the common man and seeker of truth, entered into an intense struggle with the base nature of the Gollum shadow, more interested in possessiveness and dominion over life at his level of society and culture than letting go. He lost the struggle, only to be redeemed by a higher will. According to palmistry, the third finger represents the god, Apollo and symbolizes the sun of consciousness and the concomitant ego-will that needed to be sacrificed for the sake of a higher truth. It is as if to say that, at the last moment, overwhelmed by his Gollum shadow, Frodo became possessed by the will-to-power, which

---

[200] Tolkien, 2005b
[201] Verlyn Flieger, 1983, p. 154

led to the, apparently unwilling, act of sacrifice. In a letter, according to Tolkien, [Gollum] did rob and injure [Frodo] in the end – but by 'grace,' that last betrayal was at a precise juncture when the final evil deed was the most beneficial thing anyone cd. have done for Frodo."[202] Frodo's objective awareness of his subjectivity, including his demonstrated weakness at the crucial moment and the unwilling sacrifice of his finger, along with the descent of grace, brought redemption.

After the destruction of the Ring, Frodo eventually returned to the Shire for the next three years and wrote out the story of the War of the Rings as his contribution to the Red Book of Westmarch, which included a portion from Bilbo, leaving the final pages to Sam. According to a poem called *Sea-Bell* that Tolkien ascribed to Frodo by having a pseudo-editor scrawl at its head, *Frodo's Dreme*, Frodo ended his days in the Shire with the loss of joy and meaning of life.[203] The poem expresses despair, lonely withdrawal, loss of self and lack of meaningful relationship:

> *"Bent though I be, I must find the sea!*
> *I have lost myself, and know not the way...*
> *.....*
> *Never will my ear that bell hear*
> *never my feet that shore tread*
> *never again, as in sad lane,*
> *in blind alley and in long street*
> *ragged I walk. To myself I talk;*
> *for still they speak not, men that [I] meet* [204]*."*

Frodo's suffering is that of the soul and psychic being in face of the human condition, which constantly confronts sensitive individuals with a reality in direct opposition to their true needs.

Frodo told Sam that he had been too deeply hurt to enjoy life in

---

[202] As reported in ibid
[203] Verlyn Flieger, 1983
[204] J. R. R. Tolkien, 1966, p. 59, 60

the Shire, which he declared had been saved for others but not for him, pointing to the archetype of the Savior.[205] Although that may be true, and understandably so, the apparent inability to communicate to others the nature and meaning of his experience suggests that, despite his redemption and experience of grace, Frodo failed in the hero's final task, which is to bring back the boon of his discovery to others. Joseph Campbell wrote that "bringing back the boon" requires that heroes return with what they went to discover, and it is sometimes more difficult than the actual descent into one's depths.[206] He observed that there are three typical responses to the return of the hero:

1. There is no reception at all to heroes and their message; this is known as the "refusal of the return."
2. Returned heroes give people what they want to hear rather than the truth of their discovery, or
3. Heroes find a means to communicate their new-found truth in the proportion that it can be received.

From a psychological perspective "failure of the return" refers to the inability to assimilate inner experiences into the reality of every day life.

More than anybody else in *The Lord of the Rings,* Frodo's path resembled the *via dolorosa* of Christ and the burden of carrying one's cross. To aid him in his path of suffering and pain, as he left Lothlórien, Galadriel gave him the gift of a crystal Phial containing the transcendent white light of Eärendil. It helped Frodo overcome his desire for the Ring, brought strength and courage in dark moments, and shone brighter with expressions of hope and bravery by the bearer.

Despite this assistance from a transcendent source, like Simon of Cyrene, who was compelled by a Roman soldier to help the suffering Christ carry his cross for awhile, Frodo received the help of Sam at the crucial moment. After a life and death struggle, he was captured and paralyzed,

---

[205] Tolkien, 2005c
[206] 2004d, p. 119

seemingly dead, by the terrible spider-mother Shelob in her filthy lair on the staircase of Cirith Ungol, the pass of the spider.[207] Sam rescued Frodo, using the feminine spiritual light from the Phial of Galadriel, her gift to Frodo, to disturb Shelob, rendering her unintelligent and ineffective, and to induce hope and strength. Psychologically, accessing the healing light of the feminine Self within is by far the most effective way of beating a regressive depression and psychic paralysis.

Later on, at the final stage of their painful journey to Mount Doom, Sam took on the burden of carrying Frodo, along with the Ring, on his back.[208] The inability to carry his full burden and his becoming paralyzed indicates that Frodo was overcome by the enormity of the task at hand and regressed into unconsciousness. Rather than seeing this as due to a serious character flaw, I believe it is more accurate to refer to it as the result of his suffering his specific human limitation and *hamartia* in the sense of a wounded vision, nevertheless, a *karmic* tendency that foretold his conscious refusal to sacrifice the Ring at the Crack of Doom and his later inability to communicate the deeper meaning of his quest.

Frodo eventually left Middle-earth, a tragic figure, along with Gandalf and the Elves for the Undying Lands in the West. For one reason or another, perhaps the lack of readiness of the common folk, perhaps because of the limitation of Frodo's character, or both, the more profound meaning of the quest for individuation and the deep suffering it entailed, was not transmitted to others and remained in the unconscious. Frodo, the common man, was unable to assimilate to consciousness the deeper meaning of his inner explorations and the terrible nature of the evil Shadow and communicate it in an acceptable way to others. In fact, Fundamentalists generally get caught through shadow projection being overly concerned about other people's personal shadow, while denying and repressing their own. Likewise, activists and idealists are often highly focused on the Collective Shadow, while ignoring their own personal

---

[207] Tolkien, 2005b
[208] Tolkien, 2005c

shadow and its relationship to the Archetypal Shadow in the dynamics of everyday life.

From this perspective, Frodo was limited by the fact that he became so highly focused on the archetypal Shadow and was unable to assimilate to consciousness qualities attributed to Sam involving humility, and Eros and feeling values, which would relate his experiences to common everyday life. Here it is worthwhile remembering that Sam, not Frodo, had the wherewithal to access the white light of the glass of Galadriel, first, in his battle with Shelob and later upon entering and exiting the Tower of Cirith Ungol in order to momentarily break the attention of the terrible Watchers at the gate of the Tower of Cirith Ungol.[209] Yet, Frodo had attained purity of being, as symbolized by a white star-like gem given to him by Queen Arwen on the hobbits departure from Ithilien and the return journey home.[210] It hung from a silver chain and had lain upon her breast. She also acknowledged that his life was interwoven with hers [Evenstar] and King Aragorn [Elfstone] and that he has earned a place on the ship from the Grey Havens to the Uttermost West and the Undying Lands in her place for purposes of healing, should he so choose. In the meantime, the gem will bring solace when his burdens and memory of fear overcome him. Frodo had fulfilled his destiny as his life had become consciously interconnected with that of the King and Queen, the representatives of the male and female powers of the One in Middle-earth. He had attained, in other words, a living relationship through the heart, the incarnated soul and psychic being, with the ruling consciousness and Eros values of the coming Fourth Age.

When Frodo gazed into the mirror of Galadriel at Lothlórien, he had a vision that tied him into a greater history that included darkness and light, storm and sun and the banner of a white tree illuminated by the sun. At the end of the vision he saw "into the mists a small ship passed away, twinkling with lights," portending his eventual departure to the

---

[209] Tolkien, 2005c

[210] Ibid

Undying lands[211]. Despite everything, then, exercise of moral choice and free will, and the fulfillment of destiny came together for Frodo. Even if the hero's task remained incomplete, he lived a complete life and no one can ask for more. In fact, Frodo's wholeness of being is indicated in the fact that, in addition to his main soul-type as a trader and common man, he embodied the essence of the other three soul-types. Inasmuch as he had gained considerably in wisdom and knowledge, including of the Shadow, and he became transparent and open to Elf sensibilities, Frodo fulfilled the priestly function. As Ring-bearer he expressed leadership qualities in taking on the burden of the Ring, as well as in his relationship to Sam, Gollum and others. On the four hobbits return home, he naturally assumed the role of moral leadership in raising the folk of the Shire to rebel against the Chief's men and their oppressive Rule, although Merry and Pippin were the two military leaders in the ensuing Battle of Bywater.[212] Finally, he was servant to Gandalf and his vision, as well as all the Free People of Middle-earth in his quest to surrender the Ring of Power.

Sam's vision when looking into the mirror was of a different sort.[213] First he saw Frodo, pale faced and asleep in a foreboding space, and himself in a dark corridor and climbing endlessly, foretelling his dark adventure when he helped save Frodo. He then saw the Shire being devastated, including crashing trees and the old mill being replaced by a new building. Unlike Frodo, Sam's mission was to eventually return home to the Shire and, as it turns out, to marry Rosie Cotton (derived from Cotman: 'someone who lives in a cottage') and become mayor.

THE SOUL-TYPE OF THE SERVANT AND MAYOR

Sam represents the fourth soul-type, the servant. Although the spirit of service and self-sacrifice is ubiquitous throughout *The Lord of the Rings* and evident in all of the principal hero figures, the person who represents these

---

[211] Tolkien, 2005a, p. 474

[212] Tolkien, 2005c

[213] Ibid

qualities most obviously is Sam. From the outset of the story Sam joined in the quest because of his devoted service to Frodo and love of Elves. His loving devotion to Frodo became especially evident when the Fellowship broke up and Frodo was prepared to go to Mordor alone. Sam would not let that happen and insisted that he go along with him out of loyalty and love.[214] When Frodo was paralyzed by Shelob, he became involved in a furious struggle with Shelob, maiming and possibly killing her, first using Frodo's dagger, Sting, and then destroying her by the powerful white light emanating from the Phial of Galadriel.[215] He then took on the burden of the Ring, gently lifting the chain from Frodo's neck and placing it around his own. Presumably Sam's humility, guilelessness, honesty, and capacity for love and genuine self-sacrifice are what allowed him to connect to the white light of the Elbereth, the Star Queen and to penetrate and destroy the destructive power of Shelob. Psychologically, this refers to the need to integrate qualities embodied by Sam, that of the devoted servant, in order to access the inner feminine and the power of love and its redemptive force of healing. With regard to the archetype of the life of Christ, Sam represents the suffering servant.

Galadriel's gift to Sam, as "a gardener and lover of trees", was "a little box of plain grey wood, unadorned" except for a silver letter G, standing for both Galadriel and garden.[216] Here the archetype of the goddess [Elbereth], through her agent [Galadriel], choosing her lover as the Gardener for the Garden of God is actualized.[217] In it were fine powder and a silver seed. Back in the Shire, Sam later spread the powder from which grew many trees replacing those that were destroyed, and then the seed that became a beautiful *mallorn* tree with silver bark and golden flowers.[218] Its significance lay in the fact that it was "the only *mallorn* west of the mountains and east of the sea", indicating both its high value as

---

[214] Tolkien, 2005a

[215] Tolkien, 2005b

[216] Tolkien, 2005a, p. 489

[217] John Perry, 1970

[218] Tolkien, 2005c

axis mundi or "centre of the world" and midpoint between both the depth of being [the sea] and the spiritual heights [mountains].[219] The tree in which the trunk became a crown on top represents an enchanted tree of life and symbol of individuation and psychic growth, embracing all life from its roots to the crown and spiritual transcendence. The many new trees represent renewal of life, which include the embodiment of values incarnated in the Elves. Thanks to Galadriel's gift and Sam's loving care, life in the Shire experienced rebirth and a hopeful future in the Fourth Age of Man. Success against evil forces now requires Man to access and become conscious of values and sensibilities formerly projected onto the Elves.

Sam, whose full first name was Samwise, reflecting his simplicity and wisdom, was not only a gardener but was elected mayor seven times. His popularity as mayor was no doubt related to his intimate connection to the earth, his loving relationship to the Elf-Lady, Galadriel and his natural instinct for service to the people. Like the other three principal heroes Sam attained wholeness of being. In addition to his main soul-type as servant, he embodied the essence of the other three soul-types. He had gained in wisdom including knowledge of the Shadow, and he brought healing to the Shire, fulfilling the priestly function. He was at ease and related to his fellow common person as indicated in his being elected mayor seven times, fulfilling the essential requirements of the trader/bourgeois soul-type. As mayor, he was also a leader of his people in the Shire and, along with his wife, Rose he initiated a more fruitful and balanced life in the Fourth Age.

Although Tolkien never attributed this meaning to the name of this humble hobbit, Sam means "God has heard," which is, in fact, indicative of his way of being and experience during the War of the Rings and afterwards, and suggests a good relationship with a transcendent source. Qualitatively, seven [7] is a number that includes three [3] and four [4], symbolizing individuation in both its aspect of wholeness [4] and dynamic process [3]. As mayor, Sam represents the ruling consciousness at the community level as does Aragorn at the level of the Middle-earth at large. He married Rosie Cotton, who represents the Queen at a local

---

[219] ibid, p. 1339

level, holding Eros and feeling values and relationship to the community. Her name Rose, a symbol of love, and Cotton, which signifies natural purity, given its white color and origins in vegetative nature, is highly appropriate to the task. In fact, Tolkien derived the name Cotton from Cotman, meaning 'someone who lives in a cottage,' which is indicative of Rosie's introverted and feminine nature.[220]

Their first offspring was Elanor, named on Frodo's suggestion, after a little golden flower, *elanor* [Elf-Sindarin: 'star-sun'], they saw in the Elf-haven, Lothlórien.[221] The name, star-sun, suggests the incarnation of the individual Self or psychic being as an aspect of Elbereth [Star-Queen] the transcendent feminine and the sun of Consciousness. She grew up and became known as Elanor the Fair because of her beauty, which resembled that of an Elf, and she became a maid of honor to the Elf-Queen Arwen.[222]

Altogether there were thirteen children indicating the fruitfulness of Sam and Rose's union, where the number thirteen [13] symbolically refers to transformation of life. Since, according to theosophical reduction, the numbers constituting thirteen [13] add up to four [1 +3 =4], thirteen [13] also symbolizes wholeness. The marriage of Sam and Rose resulted in a beautiful and harmonious relationship to values and sensibilities formerly embodied by the Elves, and a fruitful transformation of being, underscoring the potential central meaning and value of unfolding life in the Shire during the Fourth Age. Sam's natural humility and honesty is an essential aspect of this renewed life. Given our current ecological crisis, we are finally awakening to the truth of this message at least on the physical plane. We need to realize that the same truth holds for the renewal of life itself and the need for humility in this age of narcissistic grandiosity.

Sam was able to serve the community at large through love and help foster renewal at a local level, thus, finishing Frodo's story. Not everybody is meant to go on a journey of far-reaching spiritual and cultural transformation like Frodo or, even, Sam. But the life of the community

---

[220] Robert Foster, 1978

[221] Tolkien, 2005c

[222] Robert Foster, 1978

can still find renewal thanks to the wisdom gained by creative individuals and their inner discoveries. Here we can look to Jung and Tolkien and their prophetic messages for the renewal of culture in our times.

* * *

Jung has elucidated the way for individuals to embark on the path towards wholeness in what he referred to as the individuation process, the coming to be of the Self. He has also made important observations concerning the individuation of humankind and society. Tolkien's mythology brings the necessary compensation for our contemporary culture and times in a way that is in harmony with the former's vision. As an artist, he was a "collective man" in the true sense of the word and his sub-creation gives us images, words, language, values and a perspective that can serve as a shinning light that illuminates our deeper needs for collective individuation and the way towards the future. His message involves the requirement to assimilate both pagan sensibility and Christian values to consciousness, each of which have slipped into the unconscious in our one-sided scientific and technological, consumer-driven world. Tolkien has also given us imagistic and feeling examples of the path of individuation as articulated by Jung and the forces with which one has to contend. Giving up the Ring of Power and living more according to Eros and feeling values is essential for the process.

Like a shaman, Tolkien made extended journeys throughout the archetypal worlds of Faërie and reported back what he experienced to the community at large. He had the capacity to relate inner experiences to the world of space and time, making his work culturally relevant and formative. He was a genius and prophet for our times and, both as individuals and as a culture, we would do well to pay heed to his message and its meaning.

REFERENCES

Dr. Soumitra Basu, Dr. A. K. Basu. "The genesis of psychiatry in India." In Namah. Vol. 9, Issue 4. Pondicherry, India January 15, 2002. p.p.28, 29, 28-34 passim.

Merill Berger and Stephen Segaller (2000). The wisdom of the dream: The world of C. G. Jung. New York: T V Books, L.L.C., p.10.

Marjorie Burns (2005). Perilous realms:Celtic and norse in Tolkien's middle-earth. Toronto: University of Toronto Press. pp. 93-127 passim

Joseph Campbell (2004a). *"Myth through time."* In Pathways to bliss: Mythology and personal transformation. Edited and with a forward by David Kudler. Novato CA: New World Library. pp. 21-43 passim, 24.

Joseph Campbell (2004b). In Pathways to bliss: Mythology and personal transformation. Edited and with a forward by David Kudler. Novato CA: New World Library. p. xvii.

Joseph Campbell (2004c). *"The necessity of rites."* In Pathways to bliss: Mythology and personal transformation. Edited and with a forward by David Kudler. Novato CA: New World Library. pp. 3-20 passim.

Joseph Campbell (2004d). *"The hero's journey."* In Pathways to bliss: Mythology and personal transformation. Edited and with a forward by David Kudler. Novato CA: New World Library. pp. 109-133 passim, 119-121 passim.

A. S. Dalal, compiler (2002). Emergence of the psychic; Governance of life by the soul: Selections from the Works of Sri Aurobindo and the Mother. Introduction by A.S. Dalal. Foreward by Dr. Karen Singh. Pondicherry: Sri Aurobindo Ashram publications Department. passim.

Deuteronomy 5: 9, 10; Exodus 20:5, 6; Numbers 14:18. The jerusalem bible. Garden City, NY: Doubleday & Company, Inc.

Edward F. Edinger (1996). The new god-image: A study of Jung's key letters concerning the evolution of the western god image. Edited by Dianne D. Cordic and Charles Yates, M. D. Wilmette, Illinois: Chiron Publications. pp. 115, 116, 119.

Verlyn Flieger (1983): Splintered light: Logos and language in Tolkien's world. Revised Edition. Kent Ohio: Kent State University Press. pp. 145, 154, 162-165 passim.

Verlyn Flieger(1997) A question of time. Kent Ohio: Kent State University Press. p. 4, 76, 89, 156, 165,166,167 passim, 195.

Robert Foster (1978). The complete guide to middle-earth: From the hobbit to the silmarillion. New York: Ballantyne Books, passim, pp. 6, 42, 43 passim, 142, 145, 153, 217, 280, 281 passim, 281, 318, 319 passim, 321, 327-329 passim, 431, 525,526 passim, 551, 552 passim.

James Hollis (2001). Creating a life: Finding your individual path. Toronto: Inner City Press. p. 14.

Hans Jonas (1972). The Gnostic religion: The message of the alien God and the beginnings of Christianity. Second edition, revised. Boston: Beacon Press. pp. 96, 97 passim.

H. Rider Haggard (1995). She. Hertfordshire: Wordsworth Edition Limited. passim.

Jacobi, Jolande & R. F. C. Hull, editors (1974). C. G. Jung: Psychological Reflections: A new anthology of his writings 1905-1961. Bollingen series XXXI. Princeton, N. J.: Princeton University Press. p. 47.

Lawrence Jaffé, (1999). *"Interview with edward f. edinger."* In Journal of Jungian Theory and Practice. Publisher: Jung Institute of New York, Pp. 51-66, passim, 59.

C.G. Jung (1965). Memories, dreams, reflections. Recorded and Edited by Aniela Jaffé. Translated from the German by Richard and Clara Winston. New York: Vintage Books. pp. 182, 182-185 passim, 311, 340, 389.

C. G. Jung (editor) (1964). Man and his symbols. (With Marie Louise von Franz, Joseph L. Henderson, Jolande Jacobi, Aniela Jaffé.) London: Aldus Books.

C. G. Jung (1966). *"Psychology and literature."* In The Spirit in man art and literature. Translated by R.F.C. Hull. London: Routledge & Kegan, Paul. pp. 84-105, p. 101.

C. G. Jung (1970a). The Collected Works. "The undiscovered self (present and future)." In Civilization in transition. Bollingen Series XX. Volume 10. Translated by R. F. C. Hull. Princeton NJ: Princeton University Press. p. 304.

C. G. Jung (1970b). Collected Works. "Wotan", "After the catastrophe". In Civilization in transition. Bollingen Series XX. Volume 10. Translated by R. F. C. Hull. Princeton NJ: Princeton University Press. pp. 179-193 passim, 194-217 passim.

C. G. Jung (1974a). The Collected Works. 19 volumes. Volume 14. Mysterium Coniunctionis. Translated by R. F. C. Hull. Bollingen Series XX. Princeton NJ: Princeton University Press. p. 180.

C. G. Jung (1974b). The Collected Works. 19 volumes. Volume 17. *"The development of personality.* In The development of personality. Translated by R. F. C. Hull. Bollingen Series XX. Princeton NJ: Princeton University Press. pp. 165-186 passim, 180, 181.

C. G. Jung (1975a). Collected Works. "Psychology and religion." In Psychology and religion. Bollingen Series XX. Volume 11. Part One. Translated by R. F. C. Hull. Princeton NJ: Princeton University Press. p. 89.

C. G. Jung (1975b). Collected Works. "The transcendent function." In The structure and dynamics of the psyche. Bollingen Series XX. Volume 8. Translated by R. F. C. Hull. Princeton NJ: Princeton University Press. p.p. 67-91 passim.

Paul H. Kocker (1972). Master of middle Earth: The fiction of J.R.R. Tolkien. New York: Ballantyne Books. pp. 130,142, 149,150.

Peter J. Kreeft (2005). The philosophy of tolkien: The worldview behind the lord of the rings. San Francisco: Ignatius Press. p. 76

Timothy R. O'Neil (1979). The individuated hobbit: Jung, Tolkien and the archetypes of middle-earth. Boston: Houghton Mifflin Company. pp. 88, 102, 131, 157, 129-152 passim, 150-152 passim.

Joseph Pearce (1998): Tolkien: Man and myth: A literary life. San Francisco: Ignatius Press. pp. xii, 1, 3, 5, 1-10 passim, 12, 91, 105, 110, 153.

John Weir Perry (1970). Lord of the four quarters: Myths of the royal father. With a Foreward by Alan W. Watts. New York: The Macmillan Company. pp.22, 69-71passim.

Fleming Rutledge (2004). The Battle for middle-earth: Tolkien's divine design in the lord of the rings. Grand Rapids, Michigan: Wm. B. Eerdmans Publishing Co. p. 187.

Sri Aurobindo and the Mother (1997). The Psychic Being: Soul: Its nature, mission and evolution: Selection from the works of Sri Aurobindo and the Mother. Pondicherry: Sri Aurobindo Ashram, Publications Department. passim.

V. Madhusudan Reddy (1983). Yoga of the rishis: The upanishadic approach to death and immortality. Pondicherry: Institute of human study. Passim.

J. R. R. Tolkien (1979). *"On Fairy-Stories."* In Tree and leaf. London: Unwin Paperbacks. pp. 7-79 passim, p. 59.

J. R. R. Tolkien (1981). The letters of J.R.R. Tolkien. Letter 142. Humphrey Carpenter. With the assistance of Christopher Tolkien. London: Harper Collins Publisher. pp. 172, 171-173 passim.

J. R. R. Tolkien (1966). *"The adventures of tom bombadill and other verses from the red Book."* In The Tolkien reader. *Illustrations by Pauline Baynes.* New York: Ballantine Books Inc. pp. 57-60 passim, 50, 60 passim.

J. R. R. Tolkien (1999a). The hobbit: or there and back again. paperback edition. Hammersmith, London: Harper Collins *Publishers.*

J. R. R. Tolkien (1999b). The silmarillion. paperback edition. Hammersmith, London: Harper Collins *Publishers.* pp. v-ix, passim, p. viii, pp. 13-22 passim, 37-42 passim.

J.R.R. Tolkien (2005a). The lord of the rings: The fellowship of the rings. part 1. paperback edition. Hammersmith, London: Harper Collins *Publishers.* pp. 81, 82, 224, 254-256 passim, 289, 291, 321, 342, 353, 336, 408, 430-432 passim, 448, 471, 472, 473, 474, 475, 476, 489, 490, 491, 515-531 passim, 519, 521, 538.

J.R.R. Tolkien (2005b). The lord of the rings: The two towers. part 2. paperback edition. Hammersmith, London: Harper Collins *Publishers.* pp. 547-577 passim, 578-599 passim, 597, 610, 636-659 passim, 654-656 passim, 767-784 passim, 787-809 passim, 932, 954-955 passim, 956-971 passim.

J.R.R. Tolkien (2005c). The lord of the rings: The return of the king. paperback edition. Hammersmith, London: Harper Collins *Publishers.* pp. 1004, 1033, 1034 passim, 1049, 1098-1112 passim, 1113-1122,

1123-1140, 1129, 1173-1197 passim, 1249, 1276, 1241-1254 passim, 1150, 1230, 1271-1274 passim, 1275-1294 passim, 1306-1335, passim, 1324, 1339, 1343, 1346, 1387.

Marie-Louise von Franz (1975). C. G. Jung: His Myth in our time. Translated form the German by William H. Kennedy. New York: Putnam's Sons, for the C. G. Jung Foundation for Analytical Psychology. P. 216, 272-287 passim, 278, 281.

Marie-Louise von Franz (1980). The psychological meaning of Redemption motives in fairytales. Toronto: Inner City Press. pp. 7-18, passim.

George Weigel (2005). The cube and the cathedral: Europe, America, and politics without God. New York: Basic Books. pp. 41-48 passim.

Ralph C. Woods (2003) The Gospel according to Tolkien: Visions of the Kingdom in Middle-earth. Louiseville: Westmininister John Knox Press. passim.

JUNG ON RELIGION, GNOSTICISM, HIS ENCOUNTER WITH THE EAST, AND ALCHEMY

David Johnston

ABSTRACT

In this paper I briefly survey the importance that Jung placed on the religious instinct, his life long engagement with Christianity, as well as his abiding interest in Gnosticism, his encounter with the East, and his discovery of the Grail tradition and alchemy. I also look at Jung's observations on Nazism, his realization of the living God and concept of the *unus mundus*. Jung sees Christianity as an ailing religion in need of healing. From his studies of the East, he gains much supportive knowledge that affirms his own empirical findings and personal experiences. While in India he realizes that his mission is to provide healing for the Western soul, which he understands requires compensatory truths for its Christian worldview that he particularly uncovers in Gnosticism, medieval alchemy, and the Grail tradition.

JUNG ON RELIGION, GNOSTICISM, HIS ENCOUNTER WITH THE EAST, AND ALCHEMY

INTRODUCTION

In this paper I briefly survey the importance that Jung places on the religious instinct, his life long engagement with Christianity, as well as his interest in Gnosticism, his encounter with the East, and his discovery of the Grail tradition and alchemy. I also look at Jung's observations on Nazism, his realization of the living God and the concept of the *unus mundus*. Jung understands Christianity to be an ailing religion in need of healing. He regards Gnosticism as a speculative psychology of abiding interest that affirms his own empirical findings and personal experiences as did his studies of the East, where he also gains much supportive knowledge. While in India he realized that his mission is to provide healing for the Western soul, which he understands as requiring compensatory truths for its Christian worldview that he particularly discovers in Gnosticism, medieval alchemy and the Grail tradition.

Jung brings to the West a path that deals directly with its historical problems and biases, and that guides people towards an engagement with the living God. Although I don't discuss the subject in this paper, the nature of Jung's opus, meant mainly to address the healing requirements of the modern and post modern minds, especially in the West, his psychology aligns harmoniously with the yoga of Sri Aurobindo and the Mother from India. I write about this elsewhere, most fully in a book entitled *Jung's Global Vision Western Psyche Eastern Mind*.

THE RELIGIOUS FUNCTION

Jung defines the archetype as the "self-portrait of the instinct," the image-creating formative factor that shapes our instinctual expression, where instincts refer to "typical modes of action.[223]" An instinct of central importance, the religious instinct, he believes, impels individuals along the path of conscious self-reflection and careful consideration of synchronistic events for the integration of conscious and unconscious data via what he refers to as the transcendent function. In his understanding of the nature of the religious attitude, he prefers the ancient meaning of the word *religio*, from *religere*, meaning "to ponder, to take account of, to observe," rather than the view of the Church Fathers, which bases it on *religare*, meaning "to bind, to reconnect." The reason for Jung's preference rests on the fact that he believes it is more in accord with empirical psychological evidence, although the Church Father's view is close to the meaning of *yoga* and has its own validity in terms of binding to the Self or God as a transcendent numinous phenomenon, which is the goal of the religious function.[224]

According to Jung, "religion is a revealed way of salvation," that consists of symbolically expressed ideas and feelings that reflect "preconscious knowledge.[225]" The symbols behind religious ideas and numinous feelings, he suggests, function spontaneously whether individuals consciously understand their significance or not, for the very reason that the unconscious still relates to them as "universal psychic facts.[226]" In such circumstances, religious faith is adequate, but, over time, rational elaboration often has the effect of divorcing people from the unconscious source of the symbols and understanding degenerates. "This," Jung observes, "is the situation today.[227]" In fact, by and large, the West no longer lives in a moribund dogmatic Judeo-Christian world

---

[223] 1975a, pp 135, 136

[224] As reported in Gerhard Adler, editor, 1975, p 482

[225] 1975e, p 199

[226] Ibid

[227] Ibid

of convention, but a world of secular liberalism and reason. Generally speaking, that means, collectively, we live in a world alienated from a rich source of pure symbols and ideas, the result being that the narcissistic ego has such an inordinate influences on life that it has become a symbolic jungle.

Thus, Jung regards religious phenomena as a significant manifestation of the collective unconscious and, as such, an indisputable psychic fact. Yet, he makes an important differentiation between religion, and creed and belief. By "religion," he writes, "I mean a kind of attitude which takes careful and conscientious account of certain numinous feelings, ideas and events and reflects upon them; and by "belief" or "creed" he observes, "I mean an organized community which collectively professes a specific belief or a special ethos or mode of behavior.[228]" According to Jung, the individuation process takes one beyond "belief" or "creed" to "the entirely individual exercise of the "religious function"" and the religious way of life, which involves "the allegiance, surrender, or submission to a transcendent factor or to a "con-vincing" [=overpowering!] principle.[229]" He refers to the direct experience of the archetypal psyche as 'the numinosum' and regards it as an encounter with the divine. Beliefs and creeds, on the other hand, involve ritual practices, dogmas, doctrines, traditions and faith, and can actually serve to protect people from overwhelming experiences of the numinosum and the pain of self-discovery, which involves not only experiences of illumination but the realization of potentially disturbing shadow factors.

CHRISTIANITY

Jung engaged in a life-long dialogue with Christianity, which intensified during the last 20 years of his life, immensely concerned about the modern person's loss of emotional and intellectual containment in a religious tradition with its living symbols, ritual and practice. Murray

---

[228] Ibid, pp 483, 484
[229] Ibid, p. 484

Stein convincingly argues that Jung's position regarding Christianity is as a treating psychotherapist seeking transformation for his ailing patient'.[230] Basically he argues that Christianity needs to continue its evolutionary process that began with *The Old Testament* and continued through *The New Testament*.

Since we now live in the early stages of the Age of Aquarius, the Age of the Holy Ghost, there needs to be openness to individual experience of the divine along with a vision of extensive psychological integration of personality, wholeness and oneness. Jung is also adamant about the fact that Christianity's God-image needs to transform from a Trinity to a Quaternity that integrates feminine values and the Shadow or Devil, along with a metamorphosis from an all-good God-image to one that is a paradoxical union of opposites. He also regards the dogma of the Assumption of the Virgin Mary promulgated by the Papal Bull of Pius XII in 1950 and celebrated annually on August 15, as a significant move in that direction, representing the spiritualization of the body and the potential for the transformation of Christianity. The importance of coming to terms with Western cultural and religious tradition and its one-sidedness, for Jung, was based on his belief that a community's religious and cultural heritage imparts an informing collective experience that is peculiar to the society and individuals in question and that needs to be understood and assimilated to consciousness.

GNOSTICISM

In *Psychological Types*, first published in 1921, Jung first clearly indicates his interest in Western Gnosticism, which he initially studied between 1910 and 1915.[231] [232] Gnosticism pre-dates Christianity and, in its essence, has Jewish roots.[233] Not surprisingly, orthodox Christian

---

[230] 1986 passim
[231] As reported in Harold Coward, 1985
[232] Lance S. Owens 2013
[233] Elaine Pagels, 1981, p xxxvi

ideas developed in response to Gnostic *theoria*, and, arguably, Christian dogma finds its roots in the Gnostic world of ideas as Alfred Ribi argues.[234] Gnosticism, which relies on individual experiential knowledge, however, has never been a uniform movement and includes various spiritual perspectives. Some Gnostics, as reflected in the Gospels of Thomas, Phillip and of Mary Magdalene, understand divine reality to be firmly established on the earth and the spiritual opus takes life in the world seriously.[235] But, for the most part, the Gnostic position emphasizes that the pure divine is Transcendent, the material world is evil and the spiritual goal requires detaching from the world and its attachments and ascending to the non-dual *Pleroma*, the transcendent station beyond the opposites.

Jung found Gnostic parallels to his own experiences as documented in the *Liber Novus* (The *Red Book*) through various sources including Wolfgang Schulz's book, *Documents of Gnosis*, which includes material from the church Father, Hippolytus, who was sympathetic to the Gnostic tradition. Another important source for Schulz that Jung often refers to is G.R. S. Mead, and his book, *Fragments of a Faith Forgotten*. For one thing, his interest was drawn to the fact that the Gnostic's postulated the existence of three personality types, the *hylikoi*, *psychikoi* and *pneumatikoi*, which strongly support his theory of personality types, in addition to the Gnostic understanding of "man's unconscious psychology" and "the problem of archetypes" by giving importance to individual spiritual experience, knowledge and the process of individual integration, although crudely, in comparison to contemporary depth-psychology.[236]

Gnostic typology, in fact, resembles the typology found in the Hindu Bhagavad Gita, with its tamasic, rajasic and sattwic personalities. In both the Gnostic system and the Gita, the goal is to become spiritualized, rather *pneumatikoi* amongst the Gnostics and *sattwic* in Hindu terms, meaning balanced, luminous, and harmonious, paragons of reason. The hylikoi or tamasic person is the material individual without ambition, considered by

---

[234] 2013, pp 91, 98

[235] Alan Jacobs, 2006, pp 17-40 passim, 18-46 passim, 54-88 passim, passim

[236] Harold Coward, 1985, pp. 11, 12

the Gnostics as not having any spiritual potential. The psychic individual or rajasic person is the average desire-ridden individual, which the Gnostics identified as Church-going Christians, who could potentially become Gnostics and *pneumatikoi*. This categorization of Christians and Gnostics reflect the Gnostic's tendency to identify with the spiritual Self and suffer spiritual inflation, which is an obstacle for many spiritual seekers to this day.

Various creation myths are highly significant expressions of Gnosticism, including, in Jung's case, his Gnostic creation myth, *The Seven Sermons to the Dead*. For my purposes, most importantly, there are two Gnostic myths recounted by Hyppolytus that resonate with Jung's experiences and metaphysical position, as recounted in *Liber Novus*. The first refers to the legend of Simon Magus, generally considered to be the Father of the Gnostics, and his consort, Helena. He is reported to have written that Helena is a manifestation of *Sophia* or Wisdom, the "primal first Thought" *(Epinoia)*, which was in primordial relationship with the masculine Mind or Logos.[237] According to G.S.R. Mead, the legend of Helena and Simon refers to the human soul lost in the material world, and its redemption by Simon Magus and his masculine Logos.[238] Early on (1913) in Jung's imaginative adventure, he met Elijah and Salome as manifestations of Logos and Eros respectively, whom he later notes were, effectively, Simon Magus and Helena, relating his experiences directly to the Gnostic myth.

Hyppolytus reports that Simon Magus observed that a "Boundless power" resides in man and that that is the "Universal Root," which consists of a manifest portion and a concealed portion, the latter which Jung later refers to as the "collective unconscious.[239]" In 1916, Jung's relationship to Simon Magus takes on greater definition in that, in his imaginative journey, he finds himself in a garden with Christ and Philemon, and in response to Christ's recognition of the latter as Simon Magus, Philemon

---

[237] Lance Owen, 2013, p, 21
[238] As recorded in Ibid
[239] Ibid, p 32

explains that he was Simon Magus but is now called Philemon. Later Philemon addresses the dead with *The Seven Sermons to the Dead,* and informs Jung that the Sermons are an expression of his *gnosis.* Jung holds Philemon/Simon Magus in the highest esteem, painting his image in the *Liber Novus* and on the wall of a second floor bedroom in the Tower at Bollingen, referring to him in the former case as "Father of the Prophets, Beloved Philemon" and, in the latter, as "Philemon, the Prophets' Primal Father.[240] To complete the picture of his adulation for Philemon, Jung consecrated the entire Bollingen Tower to him, with the following inscription above the door, ""*Philemonis sacrum,*" (Shrine of Philemon).[241]" In fact, Jung believed Philemon had inspired several historical figures who communed with God, including Buddha, Christ, Mani and Mohammed.[242]

The second Gnostic myth that resonates with Jung's experiences involves the relationship of Sophia to the Gnostic demiurge, the Creator God and ruler of this world, which Philemon refers to in *The Seven Sermons to the Dead* as Abraxas. Although in some accounts like in the legend of Simon Magus and Helena, she is lost in the shadows of the material creation and requires liberation, in classical Gnosticism, Sophia or Wisdom is the Divine feminine, interwoven into all the intricacies of the web of life, and the counterpart to the masculine Logos. According to the Gnostic myth, Sophia gave birth to a defective being, that detached himself from her, and, subsequently grew intro a "fiery cosmic force" that claims to be the supreme deity holding the material world in his thrall.[243] With the detachment of the demiurge from Sophia, she found her deliverance and treated the latter as a cosmic adversary.

As divine power and wisdom, Sophia awakens humans to their divine origin and inner light, while alerting them to the seductive and illusory nature of the world play under direction of the demiurge. This is similar

---

[240] Ibid, p 24

[241] Ibid

[242] As recorded in Jung, 2009, p. 213

[243] Ibid, p 25

to an earlier formulation made by Jung in the *Liber Novus* when he made a distinction between the "spirit of the times" ruled by a demanding demiurge, and the "spirit of the depths," which later became known as the archetypal psyche.[244] The repercussion for Jung is that, in early 1916, in true Gnostic fashion, Jung was enjoined by the Sophia/soul to worship the "unmoving" star-like, "*one God*" within him.[245] As this one God was neither subservient to nor inclined toward the demiurge, Jung was instructed to turn away from the seductive power of the fiery Abraxas, which, he, nonetheless, was counseled to fear.

It is clear from these considerations that Jung's personal myth and the foundation of his approach to psychology have an important Gnostic coloration with its significant teaching that the psyche is the source of psychological knowledge, as was the case with the medieval alchemists.[246] Jung, in fact, considers the Gnostics to be the first depth psychologists who had a significant perspective on the unconscious, including that God Himself is ignorant or unconscious. Jung took that insight to be highly important since it "identifies the Deity with the numinosity of the unconscious.[247] This understanding means that symbols of the Self or the Deity can be realized by penetrating the unconscious, which agrees with Jung's empirical findings.

Jung's favorable view and kinship with the Gnostics was not only there at the beginning of his encounter with the unconscious as documented here, but the Gnostic flavor in his work persisted until the end of his life. Gnostic references, for instance, can be found in his magnum opus, *Mysterium Coniunctionis*, published in 1955, and even more amply, in his historical study, *Aion*, published in 1951 in his description of the Self. Here Jung elaborates a remarkable extension on the nature of the Self as a static fourfold quaternity that unfolds dynamically in a circular process, where the spiritual Anthropos and the primary base substance, the *rotundum*,

---

[244] Ibid, p 27
[245] Ibid, p 26
[246] 1975c, p 174
[247] Ibid, p 194

the pneumatic stone, meet like the serpent biting its tail. Inclusion of the *rotundum* as the foundation of the Self creates tension with the spiritual dimension such that the image of the static Self is set in circular motion. Visualizing the dynamic, rotating Self is possible today thanks to scientific materialism and knowledge of the space-time quality of the physical world which, notes Jung, reflects "the deification of matter.[248]"

Jung is a contemporary, highly educated man trained in science, Christian theology and philosophy, all of which inform his thinking. It stands to reason, therefore, that his contemporary Gnosticism needs to be differentiated from the classical variety, where, for the most part, the material world was considered to be an evil creation. Jung appreciates the fact that evil was acknowledged by the Gnostics as a potent force in a dualistic universe, and not reduced to *privatio boni*, (privation of the good) as in mainline Christianity.[249] Still, regarding creation and the material world as evil, means that it was not adequately integrated into Gnostic symbolism, spiritual mythology or psychology. As a case in point, the second century Church father, Iranaeus, reports that Valentinus, often considered the most important early (Christian) Gnostic, Christ came with "a kind of shadow" that he "cast off from himself and returned to the Pleroma.[250]" Jung conjectures that the shadow cast off was the "Yahwistic law" from which practicing Gnostics sought liberation. If nothing else, from a psychological perspective, this metaphysical speculation can have the practical effect of encouraging repression of the shadow and moral inhibitions. In sharp contrast, not repression, but accepting the shadow and transforming conscience to reflect the Self and the transcendent function when facing a conflict of duties, is central to Jung's Gnostic psychology. [251]

For the ancient Gnostics, there was alienation from the immaterial essence that the aspiring Gnostic sought to redress. For the most part,

---

[248] Ibid, p 257
[249] 1975e, pp 41n, 169
[250] Ibid, pp 41n, 41, 110
[251] Ibid, p 110

this means that the general goal of ancient Gnosticism was to flee the world and its attachments, and to attain identity with the *Pleroma* or unconscious Father, who is described as being without quality of being and without opposites, like the non-dual Transcendent in most post Upanishad Hindu spiritual traditions, for instance, contemporary *Advaita* and *Tantra*, despite their wealth of symbolism. In contrast to the ancient Gnostics and post-Upanishad Hindu traditions, in Jung's Gnostic psychology, the contemporary person is alienated as were the ancient Gnostics, not from the immaterial essence, however, but from the unconscious, which, the individual can rectify by pursuing the individuation process and coming to terms with the unconscious. With Jung, unlike the ancient Gnostics, the material world is fully integrated, as reflected in his turn towards alchemy, a pre-cursor to modern science, and "the concreteness of modern scientific thinking.[252]" Alchemy fully embraces the chthonic psyche, and psychological/spiritual transformation that includes the material world, and potentially goes so far as realization of the *mysterium coniunctionis* and *unus mundus*, the differentiated non-dual one-world. The distant goal for Jung is transformation and individuation to the point of wholeness and oneness, and not aspiring for transcendent identity with non-dual Reality per se, although that realization is not necessarily precluded.

Despite the otherworldly spiritual orientation of Gnosticism, Jung found several symbols of wholeness there that are still relevant, although requiring contemporary perspective.[253] Examples are the point, the reconciling locus fof the microcosm and macrocosm, male/female syzygies, the ordering principals of circle, square and quaternity, living water, well, river (of paradise), stream and ocean, sparks ensnared in matter, akin to the alchemical scintilla, stars, sun, Christ as phallus ("that has an urge from below upwards"), stone, fish, and serpent, and, according to Hyppolytus, the Gnostic Naassenes identified the serpent, Naas, as "their central deity.[254]" Otherwise the serpent was a symbol of the Self and of Christ that

---

[252] Ibid, p 172
[253] Ibid, pp 194-269, passim
[254] Ibid, pp 199, 202

acted like a magnet to attract and liberate disparate parts like the entrapped sparks and to ascend with them to the Transcendent Pleroma. The Gnostic Christ is, typically, an androgynous spiritual figure that had cast off his shadow, and who, as the *Arcanthropos*, the Original man, symbolizes the Self. For the ancient Gnostics, he was naturally inclined to rise from below in vertical ascension to the Transcendent, away from the worldly life and material reality, which was viewed as intrinsically evil.

SOURCES OF DEFENSE AGAINST GNOSTICISM AND JUNG

Before bringing this section on Gnosticism to a close I feel a need to briefly examine reactions against Jung and Gnosticism from what I loosely refer to as resistant quarters of provincialism that existed when Jung was alive and still exist. As suggested above, Jung was a contemporary Gnostic although, his full embrace of the world and the physical body, gives him a radically different understanding than the ancient Gnostics. Early Church Fathers regarded Gnostics as heretics, mainly because of their pejorative view on the material world and the human body, as well as the solely spiritual nature of Christ. This unsympathetic view on Gnosticism eventually led to their oppression by the established Church beginning in the fourth and fifth Centuries C.E. Although it astonishes me, students of history may not be surprised that this perspective on Gnosticism continues to affect the contemporary world, specifically regarding the Church's acceptance of Jung's psychology.

On February 21, 2003, the Vatican through its council for culture and council for interreligious dialogue published a document where Jung is identified as a founding member of the New Age movement with foundational elements that are "incompatible" with Christianity.[255] Specifically the document attacks pantheism and panentheism, all forms of Gnosticism and neo-Gnosticism, contemporary and ancient, which it accuses of representing the psyche as sacred. Jung is also condemned for

---

[255] John P. Dourely, 2010,.pp 6, 7

championing the divinity of the individual Self and, along with the New Age Movement in general, for rejecting the transcendent personal divine.

During Jung's lifetime, the philosopher, Martin Buber,[256] who authored a popular book entitled *Eclipse of God,* attacked both Gnosticism and Gnostics, the latter for hubris in their declared personal relationship and identity with God, the indwelling Deity, and pretension to be able to describe different upper spheres of divine being.[257] Jung, in fact, makes a clear differentiation between the ego and the Self, avoiding this particular problem of the early Gnostics.[258] But Buber also attacked Jung as a contemporary Gnostic, claiming he psychologiizes God, by which he means Jung objectifies God and treats him as "it" by locating him in the human psyche. But, in response to Buber, according to Jung, "Reality is simply what works in a human soul and not what is assumed by certain people to work there...[259]"

In fact, his locating God or reality in the psyche follows his formula for reality as *esse in anima,* a "reality in ourselves," reconciling the mind-body dichotomy, and avoiding the dissociation that results from a one-sided mental conceptualization of God beyond the psyche, as in the case of Buber.[260] The latter's lack of ability to appreciate psychic reality prompts him to accuse Jung of transgressing the boundaries of psychology "with sovereign license" in his discussions on the psyche as "creator of all that is knowable.[261]" What is knowable for Jung, in fact, includes the perception of different God-Images, some of which are shocking to the contemporary religious believer, as experienced within the human psyche.[262] As riposte to Buber's challenge of Jung regarding his locating God in the psyche and his asserting an "I-Thou" relationship, one could point out that Jung, in fact, has an intimate psychic "I-Thou" relationship through the archetypes

---

[256] 1999

[257] As reported in Alfred Riibi, 2013, pp. 65. 66

[258] Ibid, pp 74, 75

[259] 1974a, p 41

[260] Ibid, p 52

[261] As reported in Ribi, 2013, p 75

[262] Ibid, p 75

of the collective unconscious, to which Buber is not privy in his inability to appreciate psychic reality and his not locating God in the soul. In fact, Buber rather endorses the fact that souls have "all God outside.[263]"

Buber also reproaches Jung for psychologism in his emphasize on introversion and self-development, where, in fact, the individual involved in conscious individuation risks subordinating "everything and everyone else to the goal of integration or individuation" turning them into "functions of the process.[264]" Seriously reflecting on messages from the unconscious and taking back projections, where one's own problems are perceived in others, can alleviate this psychological danger. Buber further criticizes Jung for his claim that, through human interiority, one is privy to spiritual experiences and knowledge, meaning gnosis, which is not intellectual knowledge, but instinctually related life processes, revelation and "knowledge of the ultimate things.[265]" Buber also accuses Jung of moral lassitude and of encouraging "acting out" the shadow and doing evil, given his intense interest in the opposites, including the opposites of good and evil. Jung's belief is, rather, that it is psychologically healthy to reconcile and integrate the shadow into the Self, as a higher truth comprised of the opposites of good and evil. Dourley takes on Buber by observing that Jung explicitly states that "this embracing wisdom does not endorse licentiousness but rather a fuller knowledge of what is authentically human.[266]" Along similar lines to his understanding of Jung's promoting evil, and In keeping with his encouragement of faith and belief, Buber condemns Jung for mystically deifying the instincts instead of hallowing them in faith.[267] Jung's answer to Buber is that supreme value resides in the soul and "not I but God himself has deified ... (the soul (psyche))," which includes the instincts.[268]

In contrast to Jung's interest in the unknown God and Gnosis, and

---

[263] Jung, 1977, p 11
[264] Alfred Ribi, 2013, p 73
[265] C G Jung 1975e, p 192
[266] 2010, p 81
[267] As reported in Ribi, p 65
[268] 1977, p 13

the resulting extension of consciousness which comes with it, along with the effect of rejecting the existing God-image, Buber conceptualizes God as Transcendent and Wholly Other along traditional lines. The latter champions faith and belief in the Transcendent Thou, and encourages the "I-Thou" relationship between humans and God. It is not, however, apparent how this relationship is established without the agency of the human psyche. As Dourely reasons regarding Buber's declarations, this relationship turns out to be superficial as there is no significant in-depth human subjectivity in the relationship between the human I and this extra-psychic and distant God, which Buber refers to as Thou.[269]

Jung emphasizes that he is not a metaphysician, but an empirical scientist, who is open to human experiences without ideological distortion. It is noteworthy, however, that his empiricism includes experiences of the archetypes of the collective unconscious including the archetype of the Self, as well as individual life experiences. Jung's empiricism, in other words, can lead him to metaphysical truths inasmuch as they are based on experiential evidence of a typically ego transcendent nature. As discussed above, Jung, in fact, has Gnosis inasmuch as he has immediate experience of God in the soul, As I indicate above, In contrast to the Gnostics and Jung, Buber holds to faith and belief in the "I-Thou" relationship between humans and a distant God beyond the human psyche. In fact, Buber's convictions are typical of institutions and people who hold to dogmatic belief in the Transcendent God without connection with immanence, in contrast to Jung's immanent God that resides in the human soul.

The polemic against the Gnostics and Jung continues to this day, notably by a diplomate of the Jung Institute in Zurich and past president of the C. G. Jung Foundation in New York., Jeffrey Satinover.[270] He feels the need and responsibility to warn Christians of Jung's pagan and Gnostic leanings, which, like Buber, he believes opens up evil tendencies. He contrasts this apparent inevitability, as he sees it, to the ethical monotheism of Judaism and Christianity which, he believes, are capable of morally

---

[269] 2010, p 91

[270] 1994 passim

containing the instincts of the pagan psyche. Needless to say, dogmatic application of codes of conduct, including Christian and Jewish, can be of value in supporting the ethical requirements of the spirit of the times, but they are resistant to the exploration of Gnostic or alchemical depth of being through knowledge of the heart.

This resistance from the established Church, Martin Buber and Jeffrey Satinover point to the Herculean task that Jung and Jungian therapists face in order to endorse the nature of the creative psyche. All forms of resistance discussed above, however, can be reduced to a defense against the Self as *spiritus rector* and the soul and archetypal unconscious that serve to repress the unconscious psyche. The soul and the Self need to speak and function on their own terms without restraint, while wisely relating consciousness to the spirit of the depths. This transparency to the depths effectively means that the immanent God is heard and brought into material realization. Needless to say, opposition to Jung's depth psychology today also comes from so-called "scientific" evidence-based psychology, which has developed apace since Jung's time and reflects the contemporary spirit of the times. This type of psychology can help adapt to the spirit of the times and resolve superficial psychological adaptive difficulties but it has nothing to do with the spirit of the depths and Gnosis, and the advent of a new world

Having noted the above, there is legitimate concern about a culture where the moral virtues of Judaism and Christianity have been discarded for the sake of a morality of individualism and individual freedom (license). Individualism, where the individual ego is magnified, must not be confused with individuation, which demands a continual sacrifice of the ego. Furthermore, the Judaic and Christian moral codes are of value to both individual and society and need to be upheld for the sake of cultural and individual harmony and well-being. There comes a time for some individuals, however, when inner pressure originating from the Self puts one on a path of wholeness and conscious individuation.

In that case, an ethic that is one-sidedly focused on the good alone needs to give way to one where the goal is conscious wholeness, which requires a superior morality, where the shadow and the instincts need to be integrated along with the good. Jung asserts that unconsciousness is at the knotted root of much evil. He cites a saying of Jesus from the *Apocryphal New Testament* that asserts "Man, if thou knowest what you doest, thou art blessed, but it thou knowest not, thou art accursed and, and a transgressor of the law.[271]" This saying recommends self-knowledge; indeed, it requires a path of righteousness for the sake of self-knowledge. Not unconsciousness but knowledge of the Self and wholeness is Jung's Gnostic goal.

In fact, Jung sought a bridge between Gnosticism and the contemporary world and found it eventually in alchemy, as I indicate below in a section on the subject, which began in 1921 and continued until the end, but first by way of a dialogue with the East. He did not encounter the East naively but with growing empirical psychological evidence, self-knowledge and astute understanding of the psychological shortcomings and needs of the one-sided scientifically and technologically oriented rational and individualistic Western mind, with its peculiar religious history. He found both confirmation and refinement of his understanding of the psyche as well as reason to be cautious about mechanically adopting eastern paths to enlightenment.

ENCOUNTER WITH THE EAST

According to Jung's notation beside a painting of Philemon in his *The Red Book* and illustrated in Word and Image, Jung was evidently struck by the *Bhagavad Gita's* account of the descent of divine consciousness for purposes of uplifting humankind whenever the times become disordered and people no longer live according to truth.[272] Philemon is an angelic being that Jung encountered in his dreams and active imaginations; he represents "superior insight" and was, for him, a guru.[273] He, and other fantasy figures, taught Jung about the autonomy of psychic factors and

---

[271] As recorded in Jung, 1975e, p 197
[272] As reported in Jaffé, editor, 1979, p. 67
[273] Ibid, p. 79

the objective nature of the psyche. One could say that Philemon initiated Jung into in-depth psychological understanding and provided him with important keys for the development of his mature approach to psychology, with its immense contribution to the development of consciousness today.

From his study of the *Vedas, Upanishads* and Pantañjali's *Yoga Sutras,* Jung gained insight on the problem of the pairs of opposites and the solution as was interpreted in the translations he read.[274] He understood the Hindu path involved seeking freedom from entanglement in all the opposites in order to experience *moksha* or liberation, and oneness with *Brahman.* He could not accept this goal because he reasoned that, as the Transcendent, *Brahman* also stands outside of the opposites and their dissolution and that, in life, there is always need for more entanglement in the opposites, which need assimilation into consciousness. He also argued that transcending the opposites leads to abdication of the ego *[purusha]* and therefore unconsciousness. From the Hindu concepts of *dharma,* meaning the law of being, and *ṛta,* truth or right way, however, Jung found uniting symbols for the opposites as he did in the Chinese concept of *Tao.* From the *I Ching* he also learned of the danger of too wide a separation between the opposites, which results in imbalance and a compulsion for change into the opposite *(enantiodromia),* as well as the natural flow of life and the principle of synchronicity. He applied this thinking to the Western condition, where he believed one-sided intellectual development has led to instinctual atrophy and mental breakdown, since the individual has lost touch with the archetypal images and natural instinctual patterns of behavior.

Jung found some parallel to his belief in the objective reality of the psyche in the *Yoga Sutra's* concept of *citta,* which refers to formative consciousness that uses the mental, vital and the physical as its instruments. He also found confirmation for his concept of a neutral libido from Pantañjali's understanding of the *rajas guna* [desire nature], which in its own right refers to action, but also dynamizes the other two *gunas, sattwa,* meaning poise and light, and *tamas,* meaning inertia and darkness, without

---

[274] As reported in Harold Coward, 1985

which they remain static. From the *Vedas* and *Upanishads* Jung also recognized an immanent "dynamic or creative principle" in the concept of Brahman that is equivalent to his understanding of the nature of libido or psychic energy.[275] Although the *Yoga Sutra's* define the *kleśas* negatively as being related to the afflictions of ignorance, egoism, attachment to sensuous pleasure, aversion, and attachment to life, for Jung, they are conceived more neutrally as "urges, the natural instinctive forms in which libido first appears out of the unconscious.[276]" He also found in *Tantra* "the desire for intellectual discrimination" as a *kleśas*, which Jung interprets in his characteristic way to mean as "an urge to produce personality, something that is centered and divided from other things....an urge or instinct toward individuation" away from what Jung refers to as "participation mystique," unconscious identification with the collective psyche.[277]"

Jung was also impressed with *Tantra's* identification of the *chakras* as centers of universal energy, although his interest at the time he gave his seminars in 1932 on *The Psychology of Kundalini Yoga* included centers of consciousness up to the heart centre, and not beyond.[278] He was concerned about the Western tendency to live mentally, too high up and away from full-bodied engagement in life, while emphasizing the higher centers of being at the expense of the lower. The immanent *Atman-Brahman* concept of the *Upanishads,* which united inner and outer realities, also perfectly fit Jung's model of the Self. Jung was particularly enchanted with the Hindu conception of *Atman* because of what he perceived to be "the uninterrupted connection with [the primitive that] keeps man in touch with Mother Earth, the prime source of all power," from which the West has become divorced.[279] He goes onto say, "Seen from the heights of a differentiated point of view, whether rational or ethical, these instinctual forces are impure. But life flows from springs both clear and muddy,

---

[275] Ibid, p. 33
[276] Ibid, p. 33
[277] Ibid, p. 33
[278] 1996, passim
[279] Ibid, p. 55

Hence all excessive "purity lacks vitality".... (and) "Every renewal of life," he insists, "needs the muddy as well as the clear.[280]"

Jung was leery of any system of yoga that was too structured like Pantañjali's *Yoga Sutras*, for the specific reason that he believed the Westerner already lived in a way that was too controlled, leading to a one-sided cramped conscious mind. He, nonetheless, found sustenance from Pantañjali's *Yoga Sutras* and gleaned support from it according to need. Another concept he found of interest there was the notion of *tapas*, which he interpreted as "self-brooding" as a means to creatively individuate, an understanding he took from Paul Deussen's interpretation of *Rig Veda X, 121.* [281] One can find support here for Jung's dynamic approach to meditation, which he calls "active imagination," involving a dialogue between the conscious ego and the unconscious by concentration on images naturally produced by the psyche. In keeping with Jung's respect for the individual and individual differences, and concern for the cramped nature of the Western mind, the approach one takes is not prescribed but fits individual needs.

From "*The Secret of the Golden Flower*," sent to Jung by Richard Wilhelm, the individual who popularized the *I Ching* in the West, Jung was impressed with the idea of *wu-wei* or action through inaction, something he believed was essential for Westerners to learn, given their predominantly action-based extraverted orientation to life.[282] He also found support for the idea that the process of self-discovery is not linear but circular or spiral-like, and a circumambulation around the center, the Self. He found further support of this process in his studies of Eastern and then alchemical *mandalas*. He himself had spontaneously produced several *mandalas* during a turbulent period in his own life that was transcribed into *The Red Book*, without knowing what he was doing until he eventually realized that he was always being drawn back to the Self, the center of personality.

---

[280] Ibid, p. 55
[281] Ibid, p. 35
[282] 1970d

Jung found confirmation for his idea of the collective unconscious in eastern thinking in various places. Not only did he find it in the *chakras* of *Tantra*, but also in the *Upanishads* and in Buddhist texts such as the *Amitayur-dhyana Sutra* as well as in the *buddhitattva* idea of Tibetan Buddhism. In the *Brhadāranyaka Upanishad* the gods and goddesses are individualized subdivisions of the One, while, in the above mentioned Sutra, in one's search for self-knowledge, one traverses different realms of being until one attains ever greater intensity of experience of the universal *Amitabha* land. The *buddhitattva* is conceived as a universal mind without form, yet the creative source of all form. Jung was also encouraged with the notion that deeply rooted psychological processes involved in the *buddhitattva*, the *samskāras*, were similar to the archetypes in seed-form. Rather than treat them as evidence of reincarnation, however, as does the Eastern mind, he saw them as the outcome of a long human history in general.

Finally, Jung found support for his conception of the anima and animus, ideally integrated as psychic functions that mediate between the conscious and unconscious to the point of realizing the anima-animus *syzygy* and wholeness in the Hindu conception of *Shiva-Shakti* as well as in the Chinese conception of *yang-yin*. He found the latter formulation more relevant to his psychology of individuation because of its more pragmatic application in daily life. In fact, according to Jung's findings, in the place of following a strict discipline as dictated by a guru, once the personal shadow has been reasonably assimilated to consciousness, the path of individuation requires following the unique lead of the anima or animus within, as indicated by dreams and authentic fantasy.

Although Jung was concerned about the inner softness of Westerners and their constitutional inability to make the kind of sacrifice demanded by a guru, he was impressed with the guru-student master-disciple relationship. He, in fact, saw some parallel to the relationship between the therapist and the analysand and gurus to their students in India in terms of the personal instruction imparted. He, at the same, recognized the need for continual self-discovery on the part of therapists, as well as the need for on-going scrutiny of transference/counter-transference phenomena, failing which they can be of no help to their patients or worse. Moreover, in recognition of the individualism of the Western psyche, the relationship between the therapist and patient is essentially one of equals, one of brother/sister to brother/sister rather than of father/mother to child.

ALCHEMY AND THE GRAIL TRADITION

As is clear from the above discussion, Jung did not engage in his studies of Eastern thought naively or uncritically, allowing him to develop his own psychological synthesis. In fact he visited India in 1938 on invitation by the British Government of India to participate in celebrations for the 25th anniversary of the University of Calcutta. While there he was honored with three doctorates, one from Allahabad, representing Islam, one from Benares, representing Hinduism and one from Calcutta, representing Indian-Western medicine and science.[283] The three doctorates were very fitting in that his psychology grew out of Western medicine and science, it has considerable affinity with Hinduism as indicated above and there is also, through Arabic alchemy, affinity with Islam. Thus, in his alchemical work, Jung often referred to the Arabic alchemist known in the West as Senior, whose real name was Muhmmad Ibn Umail, while acknowledging his influence on Western alchemy.

Marie Louise von Franz picked up this thread and wrote a psychological commentary on his alchemical work entitled *Muhmmad Ibn Umail Hall Ar-Rumuz ('Clearing of Enigmas')*, based on photocopies she was able to attain through the challenging efforts of her student, Theodore Abt, from the Hyderabad Library in India.[284] Abt himself later wrote a more extensive psychological commentary on Ibn Umail's work in a book titled, *Corpus Alchemicum Arabicum* where he emphasizes his historical importance as an interpreter of symbolic alchemy.[285] Von Franz notes that, while Islamic alchemy influenced Western alchemy, Islamic alchemy was in turn influenced by *Tantra*, particularly evident in the *coniunctio* symbolism of

---

[283] Jung, 1965
[284] 1999
[285] 2009

the masculine and feminine principles. According to Jung, the *coniunctio* refers to both the coming to terms of the conscious and unconscious, on the one hand, and reconciliation between the sexes, on the other.

Despite the affinity of Jung's work with Hindu thought and Islamic alchemy, during his visit to India, Jung had a significant dream, where he alone, amongst his colleagues, could swim across the water and obtain the Grail. Jung interprets the dream to relate to his obligation to seek the healing vessel for the West. He had, in fact, already begun his alchemical studies, which he realized, along with the Grail tradition, formed the necessary bridge from Gnosticism to the contemporary Western mind.

NAZISM: THE PERVERTED GRAIL

Between the years 1928 and 1944 Jung passed through the third phase of his life's work, where he refined and published his fundamental insights on the psyche's purposive nature and its natural inborn healing tendencies.[286] He spent his time authenticating his findings, examining dreams and finding amplificatory material in the study of mythology, including Gnostic mythology and alchemy. During this period, Jung also warned against the dangers of mass movements as was evident in Nazism and elsewhere.

In 1936, he published "*Wotan*," describing what he believed to have been the archetypal source of Germany's restlessness and militancy, namely the constellation of the pagan god referred to in the title. After centuries of repression much of his darker qualities as a cunning and fierce god of war emerged, while Wotan's healing values remained submerged and unconscious. Jung observes that the Christian God was no longer a living phenomenon and regulating factor, but that the militant Wotan had become their god.[287] Significantly, unlike his cousin, the Greek god, Dionysus, who is subordinate to Zeus, Wotan has no god above him. Moreover, in ancient Greece, the excesses of Dionysus were balanced or

---

[286] J. Gary Sparks, 2007
[287] 1970a

subdued by one of the most important of their deities, the sun-god Apollo, a far-seeing god of prophecy, music of the lyre and healing.

Germany's pagan roots, therefore, opened up the possibility of a people being one-sidedly driven by the archetype of Wotan without the moderating influence of reason and a superior spiritual principle. As a matter of fact, pre-world war II Germany was heavily influenced by the spirit of Romanticism and the Age of Reason had not taken hold there as it did in other Western European countries. In light of Jung's dream and interest in the Grail tradition, it is also noteworthy that there was a perverted Grail movement amongst many of the Nazis, notably Himmler and his followers in the SS, which included a "Grail castle."

In 1945, Jung published another essay, this time on the fate of Germany and the Nazi rule, entitled *"After the Catastrophe."* In it he wrote about the need for all Germans to acknowledge Germany's collective guilt and moral inferiority in the face of their European neighbors and the rest of the world. Even if individual German's weren't Nazis *per se*, they were either consciously or half-consciously Nazi and in denial, or unconsciously carried along with the devastating events. The question is not only why the catastrophe happened, but why it was allowed to happen.

Jung argues that Germany suffered the madness of dissociation and mass hysteria and needed to confess being overwhelmed by Wotan, the storm god, and to acknowledge their ego's shadow counterpart. Psychologically, the individual's shadow, with all its inferiority, power drive and personal ambition, aligned itself with the collective shadow of the Nazi regime. By way of example, feeling types with the capacity for discriminating feeling evaluation, who by definition, have inferior thinking functions, were swayed by illogical arguments about the natural superiority of the Aryan race and the inferiority of the "soulless" Jew. This would not have happened during normal times, as then, individuals with a differentiated feeling function have the natural capacity to relate personally to individuals regardless of their racial, religious or ethnic origin as long as inferior thinking does not interfere and contaminate their beliefs.

Intellectuals and thinking types in general, with inferior feeling functions, were drawn in by Nazi values that supported their irrational prejudices, stereotypes, and sentimentalized version of life. They include the unwarranted belief that Jews, who were illogically associated with reason, capitalism, socialism and communism and antagonistic to a sentimental German "volkish" Romanticism, had seized economic and political power, and the propagation of a superior Aryan race was in danger of contamination by Jews who lusted after Aryan women. Sensation types, with inferior intuition, were enthused by Hitler's shadow vision of a Third Reich consisting of a superior race of Aryans, unable to distinguish between that and the spiritual evolution of the human race, and the realization of the "Kingdom of God" on earth. Finally, people with superior intuition and an inferior sensation function and not adapted to practical realities, were caught in Hitler's convoluted state machinery and dependent on its benefits, feeling that there was no way out. They had no capacity to identify, let alone encourage, more realistic and down to earth bureaucratic and administrative practices, foreign affairs, political agendas, and economic objectives uncontaminated by Nazi ideology and ambition.

Although focusing on what had happened to Germany, Jung warns that "this is not the fate of Germany alone, but of all Europe," observing that "We must all open our eyes to the shadow [which] looms behind contemporary man.[288]" Indeed, it is becoming increasingly evident that we all need to become more conscious of the functioning of the collective shadow, and how we individually support it through our personal shadow and inferior aspects of the psyche. Realization of a transformed world and new order of life requires nothing less.

Marie-Louise von Franz reports a dream of Jung's, where "Wotan, Tiw and Thor (a triad of the same god) had entered the country demanding that a house should be built for them.[289] Jung notes, "They are among other things the dark, murderous side of God.[290] Here we have three aspects of the same god, Wotan, who can be said to embody "the spirit of

---

[288] 1970b, p. 215
[289] As reported in Wertenschlagg-Birkhauser, 2009, p. 68
[290] Ibid

the unconscious psyche, the spirit of nature.[291] When there is no conscious dialogue with this archetypal personality, it acts autonomously and can carry people away in a destructive frenzy as happened with Nazi Germany or occurs with possessed individuals. When related to consciously, the same god brings understanding of how to deal with the perils of the unconscious on both a collective and an individual basis. As a *mercurius-duplex* figure, Wotan is also a *psychopompos* that potentially weaves a full life of conscious individuation and the embodiment of wisdom.

ALCHEMY

Of central importance to Jung was medieval alchemy, with its plethora of mythological images and descriptions, which provided him with rich insights on the nature of the psychological healing process and transformation, and the symbols involved.[292] Jung's focused interest in alchemy began in 1928 when he received, from Richard Wilhelm, a Chinese alchemical-Taoist text, *"The Secret of the Golden Flower,"* for which he wrote a commentary.[293] Although Jung had personally experienced the fires of the alchemical furnace between 1913 and 1916 and transcribed his encounter with the unconscious into his *Liber Novus* (*The Red Book*), this marked the beginning of Jung's long-term interest in the study of alchemy itself. He gathered together a collection of rare books, which contained alchemical symbols and language, which he meticulously deciphered in terms of the psyche's natural healing process. He regarded alchemy to be compensatory for the spiritually one-sided Christianity that stressed too much light and good while repressing the chthonic feminine and the shadow, where alchemy relates the Self to Mother earth, as is the case with the immanent *Atman* of the *Upanishads*.

In Memories, Dreams, Reflections, Jung is reported to have said:

---

[291] Ibid, p 69
[292] J. Gary Sparks, 2007
[293] 1970d

> When I began to understand alchemy, I realized that it
> represented the historical link back to Gnosticism, and
> that a continuity therefore existed between past and
> present...Alchemy formed the bridge on the one hand
> into the past, to Gnosticism, and on the other into the
> future, to the modern psychology of the unconscious, and
> the uninterrupted intellectual chain back to Gnosticism,
> gave substance to my psychology. [294]

Thus, in alchemy and related traditions, Jung discovered the missing bridge between the mythological images of the Western pre-Christian psyche and Gnosticism, and those permeating the dreams and true fantasies of himself and his analysands. What he discovered were not only imagistic contents, but also living processes, therefore an important key to understanding dreams and concealed motifs of neurotic and mental disorders as well as the nature of the individuation process itself. It is worthwhile noting that, an important tradition related to alchemy and Gnosticism was the legend of the Grail, about which Jung's wife, Emma, initiated a psychological treatise that, on her death, Marie Louise von Franz, completed in a book entitled *The Grail Legend*.[295] The main message of the Grail tradition, where the Grail represents the principle of individuation, is the need to compensate one-sided medieval Christianity with pagan, Gnostic and Islamic values, and treading the path between the opposites.

In 1944, Jung suffered a near fatal heart attack, convalescing from which he had a series of remarkable *coniunctio* visions, including the "sacred wedding" of the gods which, "At bottom was I myself.[296]" Marie Louise von Franz interprets these experiences as a feeling experience of the *unus mundus*, "in which everything happening in time is experienced as

---

[294] 1963, p. 201

[295] 1972 passim

[296] 1965, p. 294

if gathered up into a timeless objective oneness.[297]" During the vision, an image floated up from the direction of Europe in the form of his Doctor in his primal form as a *basileus* of *Kos*, and after a mute dialogue, he understood that he was called back to earth to complete his work.[298] This was the beginning of the fourth and final stage of Jung's opus that lasted until 1961, the end of his life. From then on he surrendered directly to the unconscious and wrote as dictated by the emerging material, no longer trying to appeal to the needs of the reader.

Some of the major works published during this period include *Psychology and Alchemy*, 1944, followed by *"The Philosophical Tree,"* 1945, *"The Psychology of the Transference,"* 1945, and *"The Transcendent Function,"* 1946. In *Psychology and Alchemy* Jung demonstrates the relevance of alchemical symbolism for the process of individuation and the psychology of the unconscious by illustrating how alchemical symbolism appears in contemporary dreams, while describing the *coniunctio,* goal of alchemy as compensation for Christianity. He also solved the problem posed by the axiom of Maria, often quoted by Jung, which states: "Out of the One, comes the Two, Two gives birth to the Three and the Three gives birth to the One that is the Four.[299]" This formula points to the problem of the 3 and the 4, where 3 refers to conceptual insight and process and 4 is the symbol of wholeness that, at one level, requires integrating the inferior function to consciousness. By and large, the alchemists tended to waver between the 3 and the 4, and it remains a challenging problem in Jungian psychology to this day as well. Jung himself demonstrates how the formula is solved, as indicated in recorded experiences of him having attained wholeness and oneness near the end of his life, briefly described below.[300]

In *"The Philosophical Tree,"* Jung writes about the symbolic tree rooted in the earth and ascending vertically as representing the developmental

---

[297] 1975, p. 252
[298] Jung 1965, p. 292
[299] 1977
[300] As recorded by von Franz, 1975, p. 287

process of human life.[301] Given its identity with *Mercurius* as vegetative spirit, Jung also regards it as also representing a transformative process that involves death, rebirth and resurrection, the growth of consciousness and attainment of wisdom and knowledge of God. In *"The Psychology of the Transference,"* Jung appeals to a series of alchemical images and descriptions from the alchemical text, *"Rosarium Philosophorum,"* in order to elucidate the transference phenomenon, especially as it transpires in an in-depth therapeutic container.[302]

Jung argues that inasmuch as the patient comes with an activated unconscious, the corresponding material is potentially activated in the therapist. As he envisions it, the therapeutic task for therapists, therefore, is to accept the human bond of the therapeutic relationship and to work on their own soul. Moreover, the process depicted in the pictures, which terminate in the union of King and Queen, corresponds to the developmental process in the patient's unconscious that aims at the anima-animus *syzygy*. In *"The Transcendent Function"* Jung discusses the way to come to terms with new adaptive requirements, and the need to bring the conscious and disturbed unconscious into harmony.[303] According to Jung, this requires first becoming aware of the unconscious compensatory reaction and then, holding two emotionally charged positions, the original conscious and formerly unconscious positions, in consciousness. The resulting energy-laden tension, he argues, creates a living third thing as the conflict resolves itself in a new level of being.

THE LIVING GOD AND *UNUS MUNDUS*

In 1959, Jung was asked during a BBC interview with John Freeman on the radio series "Face to Face," if he believed in God's existence, and, after some pause, he replied, "I don't need to believe – I know," by which he felt the need to later insist, that what he meant is that he experiences

---

[301] Jung, 1970e
[302] Jung, 1970c
[303] 1975b

the God-image as a greater Will that crosses his path and maneuvers his fate favorably or otherwise.[304] To put his notion of the Western God-image in perspective, Jung writes that "the real history of the world seems to be the progressive incarnation of the deity," which suggests that not only conscious individuals are subject to a greater will of the emerging God-image crossing their path, but so are civilizations and cultures, especially evident in times of major cultural transition like today.[305]

Given his intense involvement in the life of his times and his engagement at the level of Western and world culture, Jung's work and personal submission to the God-image is relevant to everybody. The last dream he was able to report, which took place a few days before his death, is indicative of the full extent of his individuation and spiritualization. "He saw a great round stone in a high place, a barren square, and on it were engraved the words: "And this shall be a sign unto you of Wholeness and oneness." Then he saw many vessels to the right in an open square and a quadrangle of trees whose roots reached around the earth and enveloped him and among the roots golden threads were glittering.[306]" The only comment on the dream that Marie Louise von Franz felt the need of making was that "When the *Tao*, the meaning of the world and eternal life are attained, the Chinese say: "Long life flowers with the essence of the stone and the brightness of gold.[307]"" According to the dream, Jung had attained Wholeness and Oneness and individual differentiation at the level of the rhizome below the roots of the trees.

The extent of Jung's knowledge of a living God is also, to some degree, expressed in his all his writings, but especially in his last three works. His three most important publications include *Aion*, 1951, published when he was 76, *Answer to Job*, published in 1952, at 77, and his *magnum opus*, *Mysterium Coniunctionis*, his last book, published in 1955, when he was 80. In *Aion*, Jung describes the progressive unfolding of the archetype of the

---

[304] Gerhard Adler, editor, 1973, p. 521
[305] As reported in Edward F. Edinger, 1996, p. 119
[306] 1975, p. 287
[307] Ibid

God-image or the Self during the Christian aeon, the Age of Pisces.[308] His discussion includes his observation that the image of Christ is all good and all light and that the shadow element remains with Satan as the Adversary and Antichrist who, according to early tradition would return after 1000 years. Astrology symbolically depicts the Age of Pisces as the Two Fishes, one, representing Christ, swimming vertically, the other, representing the Antichrist, swimming horizontally. This, notes Jung, accords with the psychological law of *enantiodromia*, change into the opposites and, since the Renaissance, the seed was planted for the materialistic world of today that is anything but Christian.

But wholeness requires integration of both sides of the Self, the light and the dark, and spirituality needs to include the horizontal and earthly dimension of life as well as the spiritual dimension per se. Jung believes that in Christianity the "archetype of the Self is hopelessly split into two irreconcilable halves, leading ultimately to a metaphysical dualism" the separation of those who belong to the City of God and the damned.[309] Not only does the new God-image, which is a paradoxical God, embrace all dimensions of being, but individuals, according to Jung, are now required to consciously individuate to the point of assuming the role and responsibility of a Christ in terms of being a mediator between God and the world.[310] Not only does Jung clarity his concepts of the anima, the animus and the shadow, but he brings unprecedented differentiation to his understanding of the archetype of the Self, which he sees as both static and a dynamic circular process. He also defines the Self structurally as a fourfold quaternity, which, for humans, has a spiritual, animal, vegetative and inorganic [material] dimensions, thus involving all aspects of life.

Jung continues this dialogue on the Christian epoch in his most passionate and controversial and, some say, most important book, *Answer to Job*,[311] He addresses the problem of good and evil, noting that Job was more moral than

---

[308] 1975c

[309] Ibid, p. 42

[310] ibid, p. 255

[311] 1975d

the amoral God of the *Hebrew Testament* that confronted and tested him. Jung deliberately takes an anthropomorphic view arguing that God's answer to Job was to incarnate as the all-good Christ, suggesting that, initiated by Christ, God now wants continuing incarnation as man, beginning with Christ. Continuing a theme he discusses early on at the beginning of *The Red Book,* in a section entitled "The Way of what is to Come," he prophesizes the emerging aeon with a new god-image based on openness to the down flow of the Holy Spirit, the union of opposites and the *coniunctio*.

Lance Owens makes the astute comment that *Answer to Job is,* in fact, a contemporary Gnostic Myth, referring to Shamdasani's observation that it relates to the theology of *The Red Book*.[312] He points out that it is Jung's articulation of the Gnostic myth of Sophia and the demiurge and that humankind stands at a turning point where it needs Sophia, whom Jung sees as having returned in the dogmatic pronouncement by Pope Pius Xii in 1950, of the assumption of the Virgin Mary. As Jung writes in *Answer to Job,* "we also need the Wisdom (Sophia) that Job was seeking," for birth of "the higher and complete man.[313]" Indeed, some forty years earlier, in *The Red Book,* Jung writes about his God-given vocation and challenging task along these very lines that fulfilling redeems him.

> To give birth to the ancient in a new time is creation. This
> is the creation of the new, and that redeems me. Salvation
> is the resolution of the task. The task is to give birth to the
> old in a new time.[314]

Jung ends his book, *Answer to Job,* with the observation that we now live in the age of the Holy Spirit and that "the indwelling of the Holy Ghost, the third Divine Person, in man, brings about a Christification of many, and the question then arises whether these many are all complete God-men." Considering the problem of inflation that this state of affairs inevitably

---

[312] 2010, p. 31
[313] 1975 d, p 457
[314] 2009, p. 311

invokes, he refers to Paul's "thorn in the flesh," and surrenders to these inspiring words: "even the enlightened person remains what he is, and is never more than his own limited ego *[purusha]* before the One who dwells within him, whose form has no knowable boundaries, who encompasses him on all sides, fathomless as the abysms of the earth and vast as the sky.[315]"

All the themes examined in Jung's alchemical studies, as well as his later works, are evident in *Mysterium Coniunctionis*, where he continues his interpretation of alchemical classics for purposes of elucidating the nature of the symbolism, goal and later stages of the individuation process.[316] The book's subtitle, "An Inquiry into the Separation and Synthesis of Psychic Opposites in Alchemy," is indicative of the subject matter and alludes to its importance to the student of personality integration. The alchemical opus first involves the need for discernment through separation, in an alchemical operation known as *separatio*, and subsequently a conscious synthesis, symbolized by the major *coniunctio* of the King and the Queen, the masculine and feminine principles.

Jung begins by taking the reader through the preceding stages of dissociation involving the alchemical chaos or *prima materia*, through intermediate stages to the reconciliation of opposites in the *lapis philosophorum*, the philosopher's stone, a symbol of the Self and psychic totality. Throughout his study, he makes important allusions to the *filius philosophorum*, the son the philosopher, child of the alchemical opus and the chthonic mother, who is "the secret hidden in matter and "the light above all lights,'" a being who "ascends and descends and unites Below with Above," thus "gaining a new power that carries its effects over into everyday life.[317]" Indeed, for Jung, psychological transformation is "a notable advance…only if the centre experienced is a *spitritus rector* of everyday life.[318]" Conscious relationship to the *filius philosophorum* and the

---

[315] ibid, p. 470
[316] Jung, 1974
[317] Ibid, pp. 41, 228
[318] Ibid, p. 544

chthonic mother, take the process of transformation to greater heights and depths of being than otherwise is the case, while insisting on its concrete reality.

Following the alchemist, Gerhard Dorn, Jung describes three stages of conjunction: the first being the *unio mentalis*, meaning conceptual and aesthetic understanding, the second, which includes the body, being the realization of one's understanding in life and, the third stage, the *unus mundus*, which Jung writes "is universal: it is the relation or identity of the personal with the suprapersonal *atman*, and of the individual *tao* with the universal *tao*.[319]" As the cosmic Self and center of the manifest world, the *unus mundus* assumes unity in multiplicity or multiplicity in a unified field, and it is, accordingly, the living source of synchronistic experiences. In Jung's words "if *mandala* symbolism is the psychological equivalent of the *unus mundus*, then synchronicity is the para-psychological equivalent.[320]"

****

It should be evident from this survey that in the deeper realm of Jung's work the religious function and spiritual values are front and centre, most importantly studied within the context of the Western psyche and its peculiar biases and needs. He has the particular merit of bringing to consciousness for the contemporary Western mind compensatory values to Christianity that he found in Gnosticism, alchemy and the East. As such he shows the way for in-depth healing of the ailing Western soul and the spiritual transformation of being required in the new aeon. Jung's approach to depth psychology is a genuine synthesis that first required the maturation of the subjective self-reflecting mind and the advancement of scientific materialism in order to be possible.

---

[319] Ibid, p. 535
[320] 1974, p. 464

REFERENCES

Abt, Theodore (2009). Corpus alchemicum arabicum: Book of the explanation of the symbols by muḥammad ibn Umail: Psychological commentary by Theodor Abt. Zurich: Living Human Heritage Publications.

Gerhard Adler, editor, (1975). C.G. Jung: Letters: 1906-1950. In collaboration with Aniela Jaffé. Translated by R. F. C. Hull. Bollingen Series XCV: 1. 2 Volumes. Volume 2. Princeton NJ: Princeton University Press.

Martin Buber (1999). Eclipse of god: Studies in the relation between religion and philosophy. Amherst New York: Humanity Books.

Harold Coward (1985). Jung and eastern thought. Albany NY: State University of New York Press.

John R. Dourley (2010). On behalf of the mystical fool: Jung on the religious situation. New York: Routledge.

Edward F. Edinger (1996). The new god-image: A study of Jung's key letters concerning the evolution of the western god-image. Wilmette Illinois: Chiron Publications.

Aniela Jaffé, editor, (1979). C.G. Jung: Word and image. Bollingen Series XCVII:2. Translated by Krishna Winston. Princeton NJ: Princeton University Press, Jung, Emma and von Franz, Marie-Louise (1972). The grail legend. Translkated by Andrea Dykes. Toronto: Hodder and Stoughton.

Alan Jacobs, (2006). The essential gnostic gospels: Including the gospel of Thomas & The gospel of mary. London: Watkins Publishing.

C. G. Jung (1970a). Collected Works. "Wotan." In Civilization in Transition. Bollingen Series XX Translated by R. F. C. Hull. 20 volumes. Volume 10. Second Edition. Princeton NJ: Princeton University Press.

C. G. Jung (1970b). Collected Works. "After the catastrophe." In Civilization in Transition. Bollingen Series XX Translated by R. F. C. Hull. 20 volumes. Volume 10. Second Edition. Princeton NJ: Princeton University Press.

C. G. Jung (1970c). Collected Works. "The psychology of the transference." In The Practice of psychotherapy. Bollingen Series XX Translated by R. F. C. Hull. 20 volumes. Volume 16. Second Edition. Second Printing. Princeton NJ: Princeton University Press

C. G. Jung (1970d). Collected Works. "Commentary on 'the secret of the golden flower.'" In Alchemical studies. Bollingen Series XX Translated by R. F. C. Hull. 20 volumes. Volume 13. Second Printing. Princeton NJ: Princeton University Press.

C. G. Jung (1970e). Collected Works. "The philosophical tree." In Alchemical studies. Bollingen Series XX Translated by R. F. C. Hull. 20 volumes. Volume 13. Second Printing. Princeton NJ: Princeton University Press.

C. G. Jung (1974). Collected Works. Mysterium coniunctionis. Bollingen Series XX Translated by R. F. C. Hull. 20 volumes. Volume 14. Second Edition. Second Printing. Princeton NJ: Princeton University Press.

C. G. Jung (1974a). Collected Works. Psychological types. Bollingen Series XX A revision by R. F. C. Hull of the translation, H.G. Baynes.. 20 volumes. Volume 14. Second Edition. Second Printing. Princeton NJ: Princeton University Press.

C. G. Jung (1975a). Collected Works. "Instinct and the unconscious." In The structure and dynamics of the psyche. Bollingen Series XX Translated by R. F. C. Hull. 20 volumes. Volume 8. Third Printing. Princeton NJ: Princeton University Press.

C. G. Jung (1975b). Collected Works. "The transcendent function." In The structure and dynamics of the psyche. Bollingen Series XX Translated by R. F. C. Hull. 20 volumes. Volume 10. Second Edition. Third Printing. Princeton NJ: Princeton University Press.

C. G. Jung (1975c). Collected Works. Aion: Researches into the phenomenology of the self. Bollingen Series XX Translated by R. F. C. Hull. 20 volumes. Volume 9:II. Second Edition. Fourth Printing. Princeton NJ: Princeton University Press.

C. G. Jung (1975d). Collected Works. "Answer to Job." In Psychology and religion. Bollingen Series XX Translated by R. F. C. Hull. 20 volumes. Volume 10. Second Edition. Third Printing. Princeton NJ: Princeton University Press. pp.

C. G. Jung (1975e). Collected Works. "A psychological approach to the dogma of the trinity." In Psychology and religion. Bollingen Series XX Translated by R. F. C. Hull. 20 volumes. Volume 11. Second Edition. Third Printing. Princeton NJ: Princeton University Press.

C. G. Jung (1977). Collected Works. Psychology and alchemy. Bollingen Series XX Translated by R. F. C. Hull. 20 volumes. Volume 10. Second Edition. Fourth Printing. Princeton NJ: Princeton University Press.

C. G. Jung (1996). The psychology of kundalini yoga: Notes of the seminar given in 1932 given by C. G. Jung. Bollingen Series XCIX Edited by Sonu Shamdasani. Princeton NJ: Princeton University Press.

C. G. Jung (1965). Memories, dreams, reflections. Recorded and edited by Aniela Jaffe. Translated by Richard and Clara Winston. Revised Edition. New York: random House Inc.

C. G. Jung (2009). The red book.: Liber novus. Edited and Introduced by Sonu Shamdasani. Preface by Ulrich Hoerni. Translated by Mark Kyburz, John Peck *and* Sonu Shamdasani. Philemon Series. New YorK: W. W. Norton & Company.

Lance S. Owens (2013). Foreward to The search for roots: C. G. Jung and the tradition of gnosis: Los Angeles: Gnosis Archive Books.

Elaine Pagels, (1981). The gnostic gospels. New York: Vintage Press.

Alfred Ribi, (2013). The search for roots: C. G. Jung and the tradition of gnosis: Los Angeles: Gnosis Archive Books.

Jeffrey Burke Satinover. *"Jungians and gnostics"* In First Things. October 1994. New York: Institute on Religion and Public Life.

J. Gary Sparks (2007). At the heart of matter: Synchronicity and Jung's spiritual testament. Toronto: Inner City Books.

Murray Stein (1986). Jung's treatment of Christianity: The psychotherapy of a religious tradition. Wilmette Illinois: Chiron Publications.

Marie Louise von Franz (1975). C. G. Jung: His myth in our time. Translated by William H. Kennedy. New York: G. P. Putman Sons for the C. G. Jung Foundation for Analytical Psychology.

Marie Louise von Franz (1999). Muhmmad Ibn Umail Hall Ar-Rumuz ('Clearing of Enigmas'): Historical introduction and psychological comment. Fotorotar AG, CH-8132 Egg/Switzerland.

Eva Wertenschlagg-Birkhäuser (2009). *Windows on eternity: The paintings of Peter Birkäuser: An interpretation based on depth psychology.* Einsiedeln, Switzerland: Daimon Verlag.

THE EVOLUTION OF
CONSCIOUSNESS AND INDIVIDUATION:
GEBSER, SRI AUROBINDO AND JUNG

David Johnston

ABSTRACT

In this essay I trace the evolution of consciousness from the time of origins and the archaic structure of consciousness, through the magic structure, the mythical structure and the mental structure up to the present incipient integral culture of consciousness using Jean Gebser's structural categories. I also briefly outline Sri Aurobindo's description of the evolution of consciousness, adding relevant jewels from his epic poem *Savitri*. Throughout, I refer to Jung for thoughts on individuation and the individuation process. Humankind currently lives predominantly in what Jean Gebser refers to as the deficient mental structure of awareness.[321] There are, however, indications of an emerging new structure of consciousness that is being felt in both its efficient expression as integral and its deficient expression as dissolution and atomization. Ultimately, the new integral mode of being is experienced as felt-intensity of being along with a diaphanous openness to unitary reality.

---

[321] 1989.

THE EVOLUTION OF CONSCIOUSNESS: GEBSER, SRI AUROBINDO, JUNG AND INDIVIDUATION

INTRODUCTION

The purpose of this essay is to examine the nature of the evolution of human consciousness and the implications for individuation and the individuation process. The connection is based on the assumption that ontogeny recapitulates phylogeny and that a parallel evolutionary process takes place in both the individual and society as a whole. In particular, I refer to Jean Gebser's illuminating book, the title of which has been translated into English as *The Ever Present Origin*, for his description of consciousness at different periods of history and for his brilliant insights into the underlying patterns and meanings he discovers. I also refer to the writings of Sri Aurobindo, a master-yogi, seer and, arguably, the finest poet in the English language. Throughout, I rely on Jung for his understanding of individuation and the individuation process.

Gebser was born in Germany in 1905 and he lived the second half of his life in Switzerland.[322] He was above all a creative thinker and first published his *magnum opus*, and most important book, *Ursprung und Gegenwart*, in 1949. The book, which first entered the English speaking world in 1985, is a detailed account of the history and evolution of consciousness, particularly of the occidental mind. The German title which, when translated, literally, means "From Origins to the Present Time" is suggestive in that the word origins *(ursprung)* implies a "leap into" or "spring into" (sprung) "original time" *(ur)*. This puts the emphasis on the fact that creation began with a discontinuous act and that discontinuity

---

[322] 1989.

has existed from the outset of time. The English title, The Ever Present Origin, is suggestive in a second way --- that, the source or origin, however concealed, is always present to the human mind, regardless of how far away the psyche, individual or collective, appears to have strayed from its base.

Sri Aurobindo writes a remarkably insightful book on the evolution of human consciousness as well. Its title, *The Human Cycle* is suggestive in a third way -- that the human psyche has evolved and continues to evolve in a cyclic fashion or, as he actually insisted, in a spiral-like way.[323] This insight precisely parallels Jung's observation that the individuation process appears to proceed in a spiral-like circumambulation around the Self.[324] At least according to the suggestive nature of the book titles then, we can hypothesize that the origin or the Self, which Jung defines as both center and totality of the psyche, is always present. In addition there is a cyclic or spiral-like process of individuation for both society and the individual, and there are times of discontinuities or quantum leaps in consciousness.[325]

In the context of the evolution of consciousness, a discontinuous, ever-present beginning seems to suggest that, at times, there are purposeful mutations of consciousness, quantum leaps that are teleologically directed from a transcendent Source. In Book one, "The Book of Beginnings," canto one, "The Symbol Dawn" of his epic poem, *Savitri*, Sri Aurobindo captures this ever-present archetypal moment, that begins even before consciousness, with these haunting words:

> It was the hour before the Gods awake
> In the sombre symbol of her eyeless muse
> The abysm of the unbodied Infinite;
> A fathomless zero occupied the world.[326]

---

[323] 1972a, pp 1-254 passim
[324] 1977, p 28
[325] As reported in Jacobi, 1974
[326] 1972b, p 1

Just prior to world consciousness even the Gods were asleep. The all-embracing darkness, however, concealed "an unshaped consciousness [that] desired light," "an infant longing [that] clutched the sombre vast.[327]" There was, in other words, an occult instinct that was seeking the light of consciousness. There was or there always is an activation of the archetype of consciousness.

Indeed, in the following lines, an *ursprung* or quantum leap into creation is recorded as,

> Insensibly somewhere a breach began:
> ...   [and] .
> An eye of deity pierced through the dumb deeps
> ...   [as] ...
> Its message crept through the reluctant hush
> calling the adventure of consciousness and joy [328]

As a contemporary seer, Sri Aurobindo poetically offers a symbolic glimpse into the omnipresent origins at the beginnings of consciousness when humankind was called to an essentially joyful adventure that involves a meaningful unfolding of the Self over space and time, an evolution of consciousness.

STAGES IN THE EVOLUTION OF CONSCIOUSNESS

Jean Gebser describes the evolution of consciousness that includes five distinct structures of consciousness, with quantum leaps between them.[329] Each structure of awareness comes in what he refers to as an efficient and a deficient mode of organization. A brief discussion on each of these psychic dispositions now follows.

---

[327] Ibid, p 2
[328] Ibid, p 2
[329] 1989, pp 1-274 passim

THE ARCHAIC STRUCTURE OF CONSCIOUSNESS

As suggested above, in the distant reaches of time, humankind lived in what Gebser calls "the origin" with its archaic structure of consciousness. It was, according to the author's speculations, a zero-dimensional world similar to the Biblical paradise, a time of complete *participation mystique*, or full identity and non-differentiation between humankind and the universe. During this time the soul was dormant and unaware of dreams, without any capacity for self-reflection; it was a time without dualistic opposition or even polarity.

If such a time ever really existed in its efficient form, one can imagine archaic people living something like sophisticated animals in their natural habitat, in perfect harmony with the instincts or fixed patterns of action. If there were such a thing as a deficient form of the archaic structure, it would be during periods of torpor and almost complete inertia combined with times of restless agitation and activity. It is a structure of consciousness that contemporary individuals can, to a degree, relate to when they are drawn into a state of participation mystique and creative unconsciousness. It ends with a constellation of the Self --- when "the Gods awake" that comes with a feeling of wholeness and illuminating insight.[330] But the most immediate experience of this psychic condition, although largely unconscious, may take place during early childhood when the child is still psychologically contained in the mother.

According to the Mother, there actually was a time before the Biblical Fall of a paradise on earth that is recorded in the earth's memory.[331] She lays claim to having experienced this state of consciousness on several occasions and describes it as a natural out-flowering of animal life, simple, luminous, spontaneous and extremely beautiful. There was, she observes, none of our preoccupations, nor any oppositions or contradictions. She notes that, during that time, "it was the first human form capable of embodying the divine Being," by which she means "the first time that the Being above

---

[330] Aurobindo, Sri, 1972, p 1
[331] La Mère, 1979, pp. 123, 119-127 passim

and Being below were joined by the mentalisation" process.[332] These early humans expressed a natural joy of living and love, and harmony reigned between humans, flowers, minerals and animals.

J. R. R. Tolkien's description of the life of Tom Bombadil and Goldberry in the Lord of the Rings appears to capture the essence of this reality in a marvelous way.[333] To begin with, their house is described as emanating a golden light that surround their guests. In answer to the question of who Tom is, his companion, Goldberry, responds simply that "he is" and that he is master of wood, water and hill and yet all the things growing in the land belong each to themselves. Inasmuch as Tom masters nature and engages in magic through chant and ritual, he is able to separate himself from nature and therefore partake of the magic structure of consciousness as well as the archaic structure. In fact, he describes himself as Eldest, already here at the origin of Creation, and his luminous way of living and harmony with surrounding nature and existence as simply "he is," indicate his essentially archaic consciousness.

Tom lives joyfully contained in song, fears nothing and is immune to temptations of power and, typically, has no pre-occupations beyond simple existence and being joyfully engaged with his soul-mate, Goldberry. Indeed, he and Goldberry are described as existing in perfect harmony and weaving together a single dance of being. She is the River-Woman's daughter and described as something of the personification of primal nature, especially related to water, as harmonious and beautiful. Like Tom, she, too, expresses herself in merry song.

THE MAGIC STRUCTURE OF CONSCIOUSNESS

If the archaic structure consists of zero-dimensionality, the magic structure of consciousness is that of a "one-dimensional unity" with the point as its representative symbol.[334] Gebser notes that the point

---

[332] ibid, p. 123
[333] 2005, pp. 161-175 passim, 48
[334] Gebser, 1989, pp 1-274 passim, p 48

is suggestive of emergent awareness and centering, as well as being an "expression of the spaceless and timeless one-dimensionality of magic man's world.[335]" Magic individuals, he argues, no longer exist as "being in the world" as there is now a felt need of "having the world" that is, of standing apart from nature and mastering her.[336] There is, accordingly, the beginnings of consciousness of human will and a way of life that has been admirably described by Van der Post and Taylor regarding the K'ung [Bush] People of the Kalahari Desert.[337]

Despite the incipient development of human will, the time of magic people is a time of relative lack of ego. Although there is individual projective identification or *participation mystique* with the tribal group ego, as separate from nature and the universe, the power that masters nature, for instance during the hunt, is experienced as coming from outside even the group ego. It is, for instance, understood to be the symbolic sun-ray that kills the animal while the actual killing projectile is taken as a symbol. It is a time of point-like unity, at the basis of which is an acausal interweaving of life in all its manifestations. It is experienced as a spaceless/timeless world of unity in which every "point" as object, event or action is interconnected with another, independent of time, place and causality.[338] It is a time that contemporary individuals can consciously experience by way of a lowering of conscious awareness, the constellation of an archetype and synchronicity.[339] [340]

It is a time too of merging which, writes Gebser, suggests not only interweaving of magic people with their environment, but an ultimate separation between the parts, that is to say the "points," and the whole, disrupting the ultimate sense of unity. With a deliberate and conscious act of will that came along with attending emotions, magic people give direction to events. This indicates another characteristic of the magic

---

[335] Ibid, p 48

[336] Ibid, p 46

[337] 1984

[338] Ibid, p 48

[339] Ibid, p 48, 49

[340] Jung, 1975a, pp 418-531 passim

structure of consciousness, which Gebser refers to as "magic reaction.[341]" Magic people become aware of themselves as a group-ego, along with the capacity for actively detaching themselves from participation mystique with nature and acting upon it by way of ritualistic maneuvers, or "magic reaction.[342]" This leads to the next leap in consciousness, to the mythical structure.

What I have described so far is the efficient form of the magic structure. A deficient form of this structure of consciousness is a devitalized attachment to magic ritual, perhaps the case of many so-called aboriginal and primal peoples today. White and black magic can both be expressions of grandiose ego power over events and, as such, also represent a deficient form of this kind of consciousness. Contemporary individuals interested in aboriginal cultures can be confused by the two world structures of consciousness, the mental with its developed ego and proactive will, and the magic structure, where the ego is diminished and, in the deficient mode, there is easy regression to *participation mystique* with others and nature. The potential psychological effect of such a deficient magic structure is that shadow complexes can be activated and, without a developed ego structure and ability to turn consciously inwards, there is unconscious shadow projection on others and, in place of the ego, delusion and paranoia take over consciousness. Otherwise, I propose, the exceptionally sophisticated contemporary approaches to propaganda and advertising, which are designed to affect people's will, desires and motivations, are based on the deficient mode of the magic psyche.

THE MYTHICAL STRUCTURE OF CONSCIOUSNESS

Although there is relatively recent evidence of people living in the magic structure of consciousness, witness the [*K'ung*] Bush people of the Kalahari Desert, it dates back some 30 or 40,000 years to Paleolithic times. Idols, Gebser observes, were then depicted with auras and

---

[341] Ibid, pp 50, 51
[342] Ibid

without a mouth, suggesting that silence and the sounds of nature were emphasized and not the spoken word. With the mythical structure of consciousness, in contrast, the mouth replaces the aura, and the spoken word gains importance. As Gebser notes, however, while *mythema*i, the verb for *mythos*, means "to discourse, to talk, to speak, a related verb, *myein*, means to close, eyes, mouth, wounds.[343]" This indicates that this way of being involves a deliberate act of turning inward as well as outward verbal expression. Both an inward and outward movement indicates that a two dimensional polarity is intrinsic to the mythic structure, a subjective experience of reality which contrasts with both the zero-dimensionality of the archaic mode and the point-like dimensionality of the magic structure.

The turn inward brings a concomitant awareness of soul, what Jung refers to as the *anima*, and what might be described as soul-time, or periodicity with its "natural temporal rhythm." Gebser chooses the circle, with its inherent polarities, [for example, the perpetual cycle of the seasons], for the symbol of this structure of consciousness.[344] In the efficient mythical mode of being, then, the soul becomes visible and audible through a silent inward turning in search of vision for outward artistic expression, particularly by way of a vision-based oral expression or poetry, for example the epics of Homer.

The mythical structure lays emphasis on the imagination and the ability to see and hear soul with a poetic eye and ear. It is this mode of awareness that contemporary people participate in when they turn inwardly to dreams and authentic fantasy -- a deepening away from the overly active and dynamic principal driving the Western ego. It is the seductive pull of James Hillman and his acolytes, and archetypal psychology, with its call for a return to Homer's Greece.[345]

As Gebser astutely observes, during the first part of The *Iliad*, the hero's moving words *"Eim Odysseus"* are indicative of the essence of the

---

[343] Ibid, p 65
[344] Ibid, p 66
[345] 1983

Western mind and its search for a sense of individuality.[346] Underlying *"Eim Odysseus"* are two characteristics emphasized by the poet: that Odysseus, the hero, is both active and inventive and the passive, "one who endures.[347]" Individuality that is to say is, in essence, cast in a furnace fueled by both acting and being acted upon. In the mythic structure it also becomes apparent that the motive-force that spurns the individual on toward self-assertion and the development of individuality is anger. The *Iliad*, accordingly, begins with "Anger be now your song: immortal one.[348]" Psychologically, these are all important reminders to the contemporary seeker. Anger can be positively directed towards the development of consciousness, and the path of individuation requires both passive receptivity and endurance and active involvement in life.

The deficient form of the mythical structure can be experienced through story and words that run on for their own sake, without self-reflection. Such a stream of words is separated from authentic vision and without relationship to a contextually significant deeper reality. It is a state of consciousness which, in men, reflects anima possession, and, in women, possession by the animus and a loose tongue. It is exemplified by a mentality that is centered on "the tip of its tongue," the spot, incidentally, where Jung put the Western mind in a sardonic reply to Migual Serrano's query, on where it is centered in consciousness.[349]

THE MENTAL STRUCTURE OF CONSCIOUSNESS

With time, the emphasis of the Western mind shifted from the balance and polarity implicit in the mythical mode of being to the mental structure, and an increasingly active, dynamic principal of being. With *"Eim Odysseus,"* or *"Am Odysseus,"* the "I"-ness remains latent in the name, reflecting a balance between the inventive, active nature and

---

[346] Ibid, p 71
[347] Ibid, p 71
[348] Homer 1974, p. 11
[349] Serrano, 1974, p. 55

the passive, enduring nature. With the mythological death of Odysseus and the advent of the mental structure of consciousness, there was an increasing shift towards the ego or the "I" along with its active propensity and willfulness.[350]

As with the other structures of consciousness, there is both an efficient and deficient form of the mental structure. The deficient form entered the Western world in Europe around 1250 AD, albeit inspired by the efficient mode that took place around 500 BC in Greece with its emphasis on the world of universal ideas. Although both forms of the mental structure can be described as rational -- the word "rational," with roots based on *ratio*, meaning, "to reckon," "to calculate," in the sense of "to think" and "to understand," particularly fits the deficient mode and its quantitative orientation.[351] The meaning of the word "rational," however, suggests that the principles underlying thinking, whether efficient or deficient, imply sectional partitioning, perspective and directedness. The mental structure, in other words, involves directed or discursive thought. Energy no longer comes directly from an enclosed cyclic polarity of being, as in the mythical mind, but from the ego which dualistically directs energy towards objects.

As in the mythical mode, in the mental structure, anger continues to play a major role. Now, not blind rage but "thinking wrath" orients "thought and action.[352]" Gebser gives the example of Moses with his anger, who confronts the Israelites with a vengeful God, and Athena, who is born from the head of Zeus, and who is variously described as "clear thinking," "of never failing aim" and as "being pugnacious and bellicose.[353]" For the contemporary individual, anger can indeed be the driving passion directing thought, especially when in search for creative new directions, and when involved in the individuation process.

Along with the awakening of the mental structure came laws; those of Moses for the Israelites, Lycurgus for the Spartans and eventually Solon for

---

[350] Calasso, 1993

[351] Gebser, 1989, p. 74

[352] Ibid, p 76

[353] Ibid, p 75

the Athenians. Whereas in the mythical mode, law is based on retributive justice, in the mental mode "Man [who becomes] the measure of all things," was put in the position of having "to direct and judge himself.[354]" Although this ultimately means prescribed law and the law courts, it was originally conceived as codes of ethical conduct. Although Gebser does not specifically refer to the formulation of aesthetic principles, this too comes with the development of the intellect.

With the mental organization of the psyche, the physical world is experienced in a three dimensional perspective and there is, notes Gebser, "a fall from (mythological) time into space.[355]" The concern with [physical] space and a diminishing interest in imaginal reality *per se* is evident in Greek sculpture of the seventh and sixth centuries BCE with its an awakening sense of both the human body, although idealized, and the facial countenance. Concerning the latter realization, Gebser observes that there was a gradual clearing up of the forehead, which in earlier sculptures was covered by plaited hair. With this development, the mind becomes entrenched in an intense dualistic focus, which becomes increasingly narrow in the deficient form of this structure of consciousness. Dualistic tensions in the mental mode are resolved by an appeal to a third point for a creative synthesis. Both the triangular nature of perspective vision, with its vanishing point, and the triangular nature of creative synthesis suggests the triangle as representative symbol.

The efficient mode of the mental structure works by moderation along with intuitive referral to the gods and goddesses of the mythic realm, along with emphasis on qualitative factors. The deficient mode, in contrast, entrenched in *ratio*, is quantitative and immoderate, without balance. Such a perspective allows for goal setting and the realization of purpose; in short, it allows one to deal efficiently or effectively with the world, at least in the short run. What we are beginning to become painfully aware of, however, is that there is, at the same time, a separation from the ecological gestalt.

---

[354] Ibid, p 77
[355] Ibid, p 77

The deficient form of this psychic structure began to emerge with the Renaissance and the exalted ego, as man now becomes the center of the universe. There is subsequently a further decent of mind into material space with the subsequent ages -- of reason, of industry, and now of information and digitalization, with its stress on quantification along with its distancing effect on the psyche. From the point of view of the evolution of human consciousness, particularly of the Western world, this seems to be the inevitable outcome. It reflects, nonetheless, extreme one-sidedness and an excessively egocentric active attitude of "acting upon." It glorifies a hubristic ego, inflated "beyond measure." In this sense it is immoderate and out of balance.

THE CONTEMPORARY WORLD

Such is the nature of the predominant structure of consciousness that organizes the contemporary, particularly Western world, albeit along with some moderating, humanistic influences. The modern psyche, by and large based on purpose, abstractions and quantitative measure, is separated from its own essence, and inevitably must give way to fragmentation and atomization. Such a structure, without connection to a qualitative, subjective base let alone the Self, must break down, indeed, is breaking down. In a world that is increasingly post-modern and relativistic, wherever one casts a glance, there is a sense that things are falling apart.

Something else, another way of being, appears to be suffering its birth pangs. A New World has been born, existing side by side with the old organization and structure, with a world view that is more integral and that includes a passive or receptive mode of being as well as an active, dynamic one. Signs of change in the contemporary mind include the advent of depth-psychology, especially that of C. G. Jung's, interest in non-Western ways of thinking and spirituality, the rise in feminine consciousness and now in male consciousness, and the general concern for ecology. The emerging integral consciousness embraces more than the intellect, whether in its deficient or efficient mode. Indeed, it seems to necessitate the recapturing of the essence of all the historical structures of the psyche, in order to live more fully in the moment, to be more present. Jung's dream of his multistoried house, representing different periods of history, points in this direction (Appendix).[356] A return to origins and recapturing the essence of the ever-present beginning, along with the essence of all the different layers of consciousness, seems to be essential in order for the emergence of the new integral structure of consciousness.

THE INTEGRAL STRUCTURE OF CONSCIOUSNESS

Humankind appears to be poised on a narrow bridge over an abyss of dissolution, which leads from a mental structure, essentially deficient, to a new integral structure of consciousness, which Gebser briefly outlines. He declares that the precondition for the new way of being which, he observes, is a-categorical, involves "the concretion of time" as "only the concrete can be integrated, never the merely abstract.[357]" This statement makes sense when one considers Jung's notion of a *unus mundus* or "one world" and the psychoid nature of the archetype, which includes and transcends both the spiritual and physical poles.[358] It parallels his observation that the archetype comes with effective power of work, that is to say, a drive to be realized over space and time.[359] Therefore, as Gebser observes, the new integral structure involves an intensification of consciousness and a "diaphanous present" or a "transparent presence" that comes with "spiritual verition" or authenticity of being.[360] Like all structures of consciousness, however, the new integral structure comes with shadow or a deficient mode, which Gebser describes as involving dissolution and atomization or fragmentation. As I indicate above, this eventuality is indeed emerging today along with the incipient urge for a new way of being.

---

[356] 1965, 158, 159

[357] Ibid p. 99

[358] 1971

[359] Jung, C. G., 1975 a, pp 418-531 passim

[360] Gebser, 1989, pp 70, 102, 269

Although Sri Aurobindo describes the evolution of consciousness in roughly similar terms to Gebser, there is one noteworthy distinguishing difference.[361] Rather than a straight line development of consciousness, he argues that humankind has been going through a long cyclic or spiral-like process, which begins with a spiritually high point, the *Symbolic Age*, although relative to later times, culturally limited. The *Symbolic Age* was a time when life was organized symbolically and according to sacred ritual. Thus the *Vedas*, the original revealed scriptures of India date back to prehistoric times when humankind lived according to mythical and magic ways of being, without being separated from nature and archaic oneness, were transcribed by mystics who broke through to unparalleled levels of inner consciousness and truth. Religious ritual embraced gods and goddesses, as well as Mother Earth and Father Heaven. According to Sri Aurobindo, the *Symbolic Age* was a time of a relatively equal distribution of male and female deities, harmony of being and gender equality.[362]

From the *Symbolic Age*, there is a gradual degeneration of consciousness to the *Typal Age*, when the spiritual urge is less dominant and folk live according to an ethical pattern and determination grounded on their soul-types. There is further degeneration to the *Conventional Age*, when not only the original symbolic truth of life is repressed, but so is the natural ethical instinct, as life takes on a conventional pattern based on inflexible and fixed dogma, doctrine and tradition that protect the status quo. The injustice and inequality of convention is subsequently challenged and disabled by thought and an upward surge of consciousness that begins with the *Age of Reason*. But reason alone does not suffice, and its narrowness and limitations in recognizing truth and determining codes of conduct is increasingly acknowledged to the point that it is presently giving way, with considerable resistance, to the *Subjective Age* and an inner turn.

Given the development of the intellect and growing self-awareness, humans have become more aware and knowledgeable about the potential for a growth in consciousness, which presently requires a turn within and

---

[361] 1972
[362] 1971

the development of an inner foundation. But the *Subjective Age* has a shadow side, which is all too apparent today. Reason is giving way and is being replaced by a solipsistic subjectivity, aided and abetted by the advent of the Internet, video games, I Pads and the like, along with considerably less interest in intelligent reading. The actual evolutionary need of the *Subjective Age*, observes Sri Aurobindo, is to progress toward a triple transformation of being and an integral transformation of consciousness. There is, in this case, a double movement,: an aspiration and ascent from below through the psychic being, the evolved expression of the incarnated aspect of the soul; and a descent from above, as in the original act of creation.

THE EVER-PRESENT FUTURE

As I indicate above, according to Sri Aurobindo, a return to a symbolically organized life, at least potentially, opens up to the possibility of aspiring towards truth of being like the mystics of Vedic India. It involves what Jung refers to as a symbolic life, which necessitates a progressive detachment from the outer depiction of the symbol along with its internalization.[363] According to Jung, it also requires the difficult psychological transition from a trinitarian psyche to a quaternarian psyche as foreseen by the alchemists. It necessitates a symbolic movement from three to four, which demands some integration of inferior aspects of the psyche including the inferior function.[364] Jung tirelessly insists on the fact that this means integration of opposites against the backdrop of a double faceted paradoxical God, both "a sea of grace" and "a burning lake of fire," where God wants to incarnate in humans and become conscious.[365]

To give a sense of what this eventually points to, I conclude this essay with several lines from the last stanza of the epilogue "The Return to Earth" of Sri Aurobindo's epic poem, *Savitri*, from which I quote at the

---

[363] 1975
[364] 1977
[365] 1973, p 89

beginning.[366] The story is based on a legend that dates back to the *Vedas*, and is about *Savitri*, "Goddess of supreme truth" and *Satyavan*, the soul, which carries "the divine truth of being within itself.[367]" These lines are, I believe suggestive of what lies ahead and the direction to which the soul of humanity now aspires.

> With linked hands Satyavan and Savitri,
> Hearing a marriage march and nuptial hymn,
> Where waited them the many voiced human world
> . . . .
>
> [while]
>
> Night, splendid with the moon dreaming in heaven
> In silver peace, possessed her luminous reign.
> She brooded through her stillness on a thought
> Deep-guarded by her mystic folds of light,
> And in her bosom nursed a greater dawn[368]

Sri Aurobindo is pointing to a new period of harmony and truth, and union of the Divine Masculine and Feminine on Earth, portending a more complex and integral consciousness, fully benefiting from the past.

****

There has been an evolution of consciousness, which has evolved in a spiral-like fashion, with discontinuous leaps between stages defined by radically different organizations of consciousness. These stages include the time of origin and the archaic mode of being, the magic, the mythological and now the mental structure of consciousness, each of which can develop in either its efficient or deficient form. According to Sri Aurobindo there is a spiral-like movement downwards from the Symbolic Age to the Typal

---

[366] 1972b, 715-724 passim

[367] Sri Aurobindo, 1972c, p 265

[368] Sri Auriobindo, 1972 b p 724

Age, to the Conventional Age and then upwards to the Mental Age followed by the present *Subjective Age*. At this point in history, the psyche is in the process of evolving toward an integral consciousness, of which its shadow and deficient form involves dissolution and fragmentation, necessary to undo the tenacious grip of the present mentally structured order of life. The new integral mode of being involves integration into awareness of the essence of all past organizations of consciousness along with authenticity and transparency to the Self.

APPENDIX

Jung's Dream

I was in a house I did not know, which had two stories. It was "my house." I found myself in the upper story, where there was a kind of salon furnished with fine old pieces in rococo style. On the walls hung a number of precious old paintings. I wondered that this should be my house, and thought, "Not bad." But then it occurred to me that I did not know what the lower floor looked like. Descending the stairs, I reached the ground floor. There everything was much older, and I realized that this part of the house must date from about the fifteenth or sixteenth century. The furnishings were medieval; the floors were of red brick. Everywhere it was rather dark. I went from one room to another, thinking: "Now I really must explore the whole house." I came upon a heavy door, and opened it. Beyond it, I discovered a stone stairway that led down into a cellar. Descending again, I found myself in a beautifully vaulted room, which looked exceeding ancient. Examining the walls, I discovered layers of brick among the ordinary stone blocks, and chips of brick in the mortar. As soon as I saw this I knew that the walls dated from Roman times. My interest by now was intense. I looked more closely at the floor. It was of stone slabs, and in one of these I discovered a ring. When I pulled it, the stone slab lifted, and again I saw a stairway of narrow stone steps leading down into the depths. These, too, I descended, and entered a low cave cut into the rock. Thick dust lay on the floor, and in the dust were scattered bones and broken pottery-like remains of a primitive culture. I discovered two human skulls, obviously very old and half-disintegrated.[369]

---

[369] Jung, 1965, p 158, 159

REFERENCES

Aurobindo, Sri (1971). Birth Centenary Library. Popular Edition, 30 volumes, volume 10. The secret of the veda. Pondicherry: Sri Aurobindo Ashram.

Aurobindo, Sri (1972a). Birth Centenary Library. Popular Edition, 30 volumes, volume 15. The human cycle. In Social and political thought. Pondicherry: Sri Aurobindo Ashram.

Aurobindo, Sri (1972b). Birth Centenary Library. Popular Edition, 30 volumes, volumes 28 and 29. Savitri: A legend and a symbol. Pondicherry: Sri Aurobindo Ashram.

Aurobindo, Sri (1972c). Birth Centenary Library. Popular Edition, 30 volumes, volume 25. On himself. Pondicherry: Sri Aurobindo Ashram.

Calasso, Roberto (1993). The marriage of cadmus and harmony. Translated from Italian by Tim Parks. New York: Alfred A Knopf.

Gebser, Jean (1989). The ever present origin. Authorized translation by Noel Barstad with Algis Mickunas. Originally published in German as Ursprung und gegenwart, 1949. Athens: Ohio University Press.

Hillman, James (1983). Archetypal psychology: A brief account. Dallas: Spring Publications, Inc.

Homer, (1974). The iliad. Translated by R. Fitzgerald. Garden City, N. Y.: Doubleday & Company, Inc.

Jacobi, Jolande (1974). C. G. Jung: Psychological reflections. RFC Hull, collaborator. Bollingen Series XXXI. Princeton: Princeton University Press.

Jung, C. G. (1965). Memories, dreams, reflections. Recorded and edited by Aniela Jaffe. Translated by Richard and Clara Winston, revised edition. New York: Vintage Books, a division of Random House.

Jung, C. G. (1971). The Collected Works, 19 volumes, volume 14. Mysterium coniunctionis. Bollingen Series XX. Princeton: Princeton University Press.

Jung, C. G. (1973). Answer to job. (Translated by R.F.C. Hull) Bollingen Series. Princeton: Princeto University Press.

Jung, C.G. (1975a). The Collected Works, 19 volumes, volume 8. "Synchronicity: An acausal connecting principle." In The structure and dynamics of the psyche. Translated by RFC Hull. Bollingen Series XX. Princeton: Princeton University Press.

Jung, C. G. (1975). The Collected Works, 19 volumes, volume 7. The symbolic life: Miscellaneous writings. Translated by RFC Hull, second edition, Bollingen Series XX. Princeton: Princeton University Press.

Jung, C. G. (1977). The Collected Works, 19 volumes, volume 12. "Introduction to the religious and psychological problems of alchemy." In Psychology and alchemy. Translated by RFC Hull, second edition. Bollingen Series XX. Princeton: Princeton University Press.

Mère, La (1979). Édition de luxe. Pensées et Aphorismes de Sri Aurobindo. Pondicherry: Sri Aurobindo Ashram. pp. 123, 119-127 passim.

Serrano, Miguel, (1974). C. G. Jung and Hermann Hesse: A record of two friendships. London: Routledge & Kegan Paul.

J. R. R. Tolkien (2005). The Lord of the Rings: Part 1: The Fellowship of the Ring. 50th Anniversary Edition. Hammersmith, London: HarperCollins*Publishers*.

Van der Post, Laurens. Taylor, June (1984). Testament to the bushman. New York: Viking, Penguin

INDEX

81, 82, 83, 84, 85, 86, 87, 88,
89, 90, 92, 93, 94, 95, 96, 97,
98, 99, 100, 101, 102, 103, 104,
105, 106, 107, 108, 109, 111,
112, 113, 114, 115, 116, 117,
119, 121, 124, 125, 126, 127,
128, 129, 130, 131, 132, 133,
134, 135, 136, 137, 138, 139,
140, 141, 142, 143, 144, 145,
146, 147, 148, 149, 150, 151,
152, 153, 155, 156, 157, 158,
161, 164, 165, 166, 168, 169,
170, 171, 172, 173, 176, 177,
179, 182
gold 35, 59, 70, 82, 98, 153
golden 34, 35, 40, 82, 83, 112, 114,
143, 149, 153, 159, 169
Gollum xxiii, 73, 74, 76, 85, 96, 105,
106, 107, 111
good and evil xxi, xxii, xxiii, 5, 23, 24,
57, 58, 64, 76, 88, 137, 154
Grail xx, 124, 125, 145, 146, 147,
150, 158
The Grail Legend 150, 158
guna(s) xvi, xvii, xviii, xix, xx, xxi, xxii,
xxiii, xxiv, xxv, 1, 2, 3, 4, 5, 6, 7,
8, 10, 13, 14, 15, 17, 18, 19, 20,
21, 22, 23, 25, 26, 27, 28, 29,
30, 31, 32, 33, 34, 35, 36, 37,
38, 39, 40, 41, 42, 43, 45, 46,
47, 48, 49, 50, 51, 52, 53, 54,
55, 56, 57, 58, 59, 60, 61, 62,
64, 65, 67, 69, 70, 71, 72, 73,
74, 76, 77, 78, 79, 80, 81, 82,
83, 85, 86, 87, 88, 89, 90, 92,
93, 94, 95, 96, 97, 98, 99, 100,
101, 103, 104, 105, 106, 107,
108, 109, 111, 112, 113, 114,
115, 116, 117, 119, 121, 124,

125, 126, 127, 128, 129, 130,
131, 132, 133, 134, 135, 136,
137, 138, 139, 140, 141, 142,
143, 144, 145, 146, 147, 148,
149, 150, 151, 152, 153, 155,
156, 157, 158, 161, 164, 165,
166, 168, 169, 170, 171, 172,
173, 176, 177, 179, 182

H

heart 7, 8, 14, 38, 42, 66, 68, 74, 75,
81, 86, 90, 94, 98, 99, 103, 104,
110, 139, 142, 150, 161
heart-Self 14, 42
Helios 22, 26, 27
Hermes Trismegistos 36
hero xx, 3, 26, 52, 61, 64, 77, 95, 103,
108, 111, 113, 116, 172, 173
heroic quest xxiii, 52, 61
heroine 2, 9
Hindu 7, 28, 34, 42, 129, 134, 141,
142, 144, 146
The Hobbit xxiii, 47, 48, 74, 77, 80,
84, 87, 88, 90, 95, 99, 105, 110,
117, 120
The Human Cycle 166, 183
hylic 20

I

Ibn Umail 145, 158, 161
Ignorance 23, 24, 25, 26, 27, 29, 142
immortality 50, 61, 65, 66, 68, 69, 120
individual Tao 42, 157
individuation xvi, xvii, xviii, xix, xx,
xxiii, xxiv, 14, 21, 23, 25, 26, 28,
32, 37, 38, 39, 41, 42, 46, 48,
50, 51, 52, 53, 56, 60, 61, 65,
67, 68, 69, 71, 78, 80, 81, 84,

113, 127, 128, 131, 133, 135,
137, 139, 144, 147, 148, 149,
154, 171, 177, 179, 181
Shelob 85, 86, 109, 110, 112
Silmarillion 47, 57, 60, 83, 117, 120
silver 98, 102, 110, 112, 180
Simon of Cyrene 108
Sophia 14, 36, 130, 131, 132, 155
soul xx, xxiii, 2, 4, 5, 6, 9, 21, 23, 25,
26, 27, 34, 38, 40, 41, 52, 60,
61, 66, 72, 74, 76, 77, 79, 84,
86, 90, 91, 94, 95, 97, 98, 100,
102, 103, 107, 110, 111, 113,
116, 119, 124, 125, 130, 132,
136, 137, 138, 139, 152, 157,
168, 169, 172, 178, 179, 180
soul-type(s) xvi, xvii, xviii, xix, xx, xxi,
xxii, xxiii, xxiv, xxv, 1, 2, 3, 4,
5, 6, 7, 8, 10, 13, 14, 15, 17,
18, 19, 20, 21, 22, 23, 25, 26,
27, 28, 29, 30, 31, 32, 33, 34,
35, 36, 37, 38, 39, 40, 41, 42,
43, 45, 46, 47, 48, 49, 50, 51,
52, 53, 54, 55, 56, 57, 58, 59,
60, 61, 62, 64, 65, 67, 69, 70,
71, 72, 73, 74, 76, 77, 78, 79,
80, 81, 82, 83, 85, 86, 87, 88,
89, 90, 92, 93, 94, 95, 96, 97,
98, 99, 100, 101, 103, 104,
105, 106, 107, 108, 109, 111,
112, 113, 114, 115, 116, 117,
119, 121, 124, 125, 126, 127,
128, 129, 130, 131, 132, 133,
134, 135, 136, 137, 138, 139,
140, 141, 142, 143, 144, 145,
146, 147, 148, 149, 150, 151,
152, 153, 155, 156, 157, 158,
161, 164, 165, 166, 168, 169,

170, 171, 172, 173, 176, 177,
179, 182
spirit xviii, xx, xxv, 19, 24, 26, 28, 30,
31, 32, 34, 36, 37, 39, 41, 48,
49, 56, 65, 67, 73, 82, 83, 88,
91, 93, 95, 96, 97, 99, 103, 104,
111, 118, 132, 139, 147, 148,
149, 152, 155
spiritual xvi, xvii, xviii, xx, xxiii, xxv, 2,
3, 4, 6, 9, 14, 17, 20, 27, 29, 30,
31, 33, 37, 38, 39, 40, 41, 42,
62, 66, 71, 72, 73, 74, 81, 83,
87, 89, 91, 92, 93, 94, 95, 99,
100, 102, 105, 109, 113, 114,
129, 130, 132, 133, 134, 135,
137, 147, 148, 154, 157, 161,
177, 178
Supermind xv, xviii, 18, 29, 35, 41, 42
Symbolic Age xvii, 178, 180

T

tamas 141
Tantra 12, 134, 142, 144, 145
Tapas 36, 38, 40, 41, 143
thinking xx, xxiii, xxv, 9, 21, 25, 31,
32, 52, 57, 74, 87, 88, 133, 134,
141, 144, 147, 174, 176, 182
Thor 148
Tiw 148
Tolkien v, xv, xvi, xxi, xxii, xxiii, 45, 46,
47, 48, 49, 50, 51, 53, 54, 55,
56, 57, 58, 60, 61, 62, 63, 64,
65, 68, 69, 71, 73, 74, 79, 80,
82, 83, 85, 86, 87, 89, 93, 94,
95, 98, 99, 100, 101, 102, 103,
105, 106, 107, 108, 109, 110,
111, 112, 113, 114, 115, 116,
117, 119, 120, 121, 169, 184

trader xx, xxiii, 52, 103, 105, 111, 113
transcendent atman 34
transcendent function 6, 25, 26,
 27, 79, 119, 126, 133, 151,
 152, 160
The Transcendent Function 6, 25, 79,
 119, 126, 133, 151, 152, 160
Transcendent One 26, 58
transformation of consciousness xxiv, 6,
 7, 67, 179
transparency xxv, 105, 139, 181
trinity 128, 160
truth xv, xvii, xviii, xxiv, xxv, 2, 4, 6, 9,
 10, 14, 18, 19, 20, 23, 24, 25,
 28, 29, 35, 36, 41, 54, 57, 67,
 68, 70, 73, 83, 86, 88, 99, 103,
 104, 105, 106, 108, 114, 137,
 140, 141, 178, 179, 180
Truth-mind 35, 41
The two Fishes 154
Typal Age xvii, 178, 180

U

unconscious xix, xx, 7, 14, 15, 16, 17,
 23, 24, 25, 30, 31, 32, 33, 35,
 36, 37, 46, 51, 53, 54, 65, 67,
 71, 73, 80, 84, 85, 87, 102, 109,
 115, 126, 127, 129, 130, 132,
 134, 137, 138, 139, 142, 143,
 144, 146, 149, 150, 151, 152,
 159, 168, 171
undying lands 61, 67, 71, 109,
 110, 111
unio mentalis 42, 157
universal Tao 42, 157
unus mundus xxi, 9, 40, 42, 124, 125,
 134, 150, 152, 157, 177

Upanishads 69, 134, 141, 142,
 144, 149

V

Vedas 4, 24, 43, 141, 142, 143, 178,
 180, 183
Vision xv, xvii, xx, xxv, 2, 3, 4, 5, 6, 8,
 10, 17, 41, 42, 46, 57, 77, 85,
 91, 92, 94, 99, 109, 110, 111,
 115, 121, 125, 128, 148, 150,
 151, 172, 173, 175

W

the Word xv, 29, 30, 36, 42, 56, 75,
 94, 98, 115, 126, 153, 165, 174
Wotan xxii, 91, 92, 118, 146, 147,
 148, 149, 159

Y

yoga xviii, xxi, 29, 30, 32, 43, 120,
 125, 126, 141, 142, 143, 160
Yoga sutra 141, 142, 143

Printed in the United States
By Bookmasters